PERSPECTIVES

RESEARCH & TIPS TO SUPPORT SCIENCE EDUCATION, K–6

PERSPECTIVES

RESEARCH & TIPS TO SUPPORT SCIENCE EDUCATION, K–6

Edited by
Deborah Hanuscin and
Meredith Park Rogers

National Science Teachers Association

Arlington, Virginia

National Science Teachers Association

Claire Reinburg, Director
Jennifer Horak, Managing Editor
Andrew Cooke, Senior Editor
Wendy Rubin, Associate Editor
Agnes Bannigan, Associate Editor
Amy America, Book Acquisitions Coordinator

ART AND DESIGN
Will Thomas Jr., Director
Joe Butera, Senior Graphic Designer, cover and
interior design

PRINTING AND PRODUCTION
Catherine Lorrain, Director
Jack Parker, Electronic Prepress Technician

NATIONAL SCIENCE TEACHERS ASSOCIATION
Gerald F. Wheeler, Executive Director
David Beacom, Publisher

1840 Wilson Blvd., Arlington, VA 22201
www.nsta.org/store
For customer service inquiries, please call 800-277-5300.

NSTA is committed to publishing material that promotes the best in inquiry-based science education. However, conditions of actual use may vary, and the safety procedures and practices described in this book are intended to serve only as a guide. Additional precautionary measures may be required. NSTA and the authors do not warrant or represent that the procedures and practices in this book meet any safety code or standard of federal, state, or local regulations. NSTA and the authors disclaim any liability for personal injury or damage to property arising out of or relating to the use of this book, including any of the recommendations, instructions, or materials contained therein.

Library of Congress Cataloging-in-Publication Data
Perspectives : research and tips to support science education, K-6 / edited by Deborah Hanuscin and Meredith Park Rogers.
       pages cm
 Includes bibliographical references and index.
  ISBN 978-1-936959-42-6
 1. Science—Study and teaching (Elementary) 2. Science teachers—In-service training. I. Hanuscin, Deborah L., editor of compilation. II. Rogers, Meredith Park, 1974- editor of compilation.
 LB1585.P46 2012
  507.1—dc23
                               2012047043
 eISBN 978-1-938946-94-3

Contents

Contents

Contents

Dedication

Sandra "Sandi" K. Abell, editor of the column "Perspectives" in the National Science Teachers Association (NSTA) journal *Science and Children* from 2006 to 2009, was a Curator's Professor of Science Education at University of Missouri where she directed the MU Science Education Center. She was also a fellow of The American Association for the Advancement of Science (AAAS), an NSTA Distinguished Fellow, a recipient of the Outstanding Mentor Award from the Association for Science Teacher Education, and co-editor of the most recent edition of the Handbook of Research on Science Teaching. Even more, she was a trusted colleague, loyal friend, and advocate.

We lost Sandi to cancer in 2010, but we still feel her influence today through the "Perspectives" column. We created *Perspectives: Research and Tips to Support Science Education, K–6* not only to recognize Sandi's many contributions to the field of science education as a whole but also to honor her first teaching love: elementary science. She was a mentor, a true colleague, and a friend. Sandi's work has helped change the landscape of how science is taught in the elementary classroom, and with this collection, we hope to continue her legacy of improving elementary science education.

Foreword

At times, teaching can feel isolating—just one teacher alone with a classroom of students. However, many teachers can also pinpoint a time in their careers when their view of teaching was influenced by observing, talking, or reading about others' teaching. Successful educators draw on their own experiences, their colleagues' expertise, and research findings to inform their practices. NSTA journals, *Science and Children* (*S&C*) in particular, provide teachers opportunities for self-directed professional development as they read and consider articles in each month's issue.

The S&C column "Perspectives: Research and Tips to Support Science Education" grew from the understanding that the literature published in research journals is not always in an easy-to-read and accessible format for teachers, but that research often has significant implications for teach-

ers' day-to-day work with students. Under the editorship of Chris Ohana, researcher and former elementary teacher Sandra "Sandi" K. Abell took the helm in identifying key classroom issues that elementary teachers face in teaching science and those that research might help shed light on.

Sandi viewed herself first and foremost as an elementary teacher. She taught in the classroom for many years and understood the particular challenges a generalist teacher faces, such as trying to find time to teach science when other subjects receive greater focus, or teaching science as inquiry when that approach contradicts the teacher's own experience of learning science. However, as a researcher, Sandi also understood the need for inquiry in science education and the ways in which this method promotes the kind of critical-thinking and problem-solving skills students need to learn while also providing them with a rigorous understanding of the science content. She had an appreciation for the difficulty in implementing high-quality science instruction and for the importance of classroom talk; formative assessment; and attention to the diverse needs, interests, and abilities of students.

With this dual perspective of teacher and researcher, Sandi approached the "Perspectives" column with the mindset of empowering teachers with approaches and methods that would not only support the teaching of science as inquiry but also the development of scientific literacy for all learners. The "Perspectives" column became a forum for bridging the research-practice gap by targeting primary concerns of classroom teachers with critical and seminal research.

Perspectives: Research and Tips to Support Science Education, K–6 contains 27 chapters, and each chapter presents an article from the "Perspectives" column. Under Sandi's guidance, authors of the "Perspectives" columns were prompted to always approach their chosen topic from the perspective of the classroom teacher. Considering this viewpoint, each chapter in this book begins with a classroom vignette—something that a classroom teacher can perhaps relate to—that helps to set the stage for the remainder of the chapter. Next

is a synthesis of key research findings, organized around a series of questions. Each chapter concludes with specific recommendations for teachers that bring new perspectives to elementary teachers who are looking for ways to better support their students' learning in science.

In addition, this compendium is organized into several broad categories, including issues related to student thinking, integration of science with other disciplines, and facilitating instruction. Although the sections are organized around themes, they do not need to be read in a particular sequence. This book serves many functions. It can be used with beginning teachers in the context of a preservice elementary science methods course, with practicing teachers in a professional development context, such as a book study, or even by an individual teacher looking for support as he or she tries to implement innovative practices. Prospective teachers will find that the chapters are accessible means for developing awareness of the research base and understanding the underlying rationales for specific strategies and practices. Practicing teachers will find that the chapters are useful tools for enhancing their own perspectives on teaching and learning, and a way to further improve their practices. For both groups, however, the power of these articles lies in challenging the notion that there is a gap between research and teaching that cannot be bridged. As Sandi so clearly understood, the two must go hand-in-hand.

Suggested Uses

Below, we share two examples of how we have used chapters from *Perspectives: Research and Tips to Support Science Education, K–6* in our own work with preservice and practicing teachers. The possibilities for how to use this compendium to support elementary teachers' thinking, reflection, and views toward teaching inquiry-based science are not limited to these. We encourage you, whether alone or working with colleagues, to explore how the research synthesized in these chapters has relevance and potential application to your teaching. Our hope is that by bringing all of these columns together, Sandi's passion for science and the teaching of science will provide readers with the inspiration and support to improve their science teaching for the benefit of their students.

Example Use: Professional Development

In workshops with teachers, we use Chapter 5 "Examining the Learning Cycle." Many of the teachers we work with already use hands-on activities, as suggested in the classroom vignette at the beginning of the chapter, but they still aren't satisfied with their students' learning. Reading and discussing this chapter opens up opportunities for teachers to consider why some approaches to using hands-on activities may not be effective and introduces them to the research base in support of the learning cycle approach. Thus, teachers are provided a rationale for exploring the impact of this approach with their own students. As suggested by Brown and Abell, teachers peruse examples of learning cycle lessons related to their units of science instruction (see Chapter 5 References on page 23). After trying these with their students, teachers report their experiences within their professional learning communities (PLCs) and compare this approach to how they might have traditionally approached the lesson in past years. By working together, teachers support one another in taking risks to try new things and in critically evaluating the impact of changes in their instruction. The chapter is a springboard for this type of professional development, but we have also found that the chapter itself becomes a tool for teachers to communicate with others (e.g., principals, colleagues, and parents) about what they are trying and why.

Example Use: Preservice Teacher Education

For many beginning teachers, the skill of asking productive science questions that generate classroom talk, promote student-centered learning, and inform teachers of students' scientific thinking, can be a difficult skill to learn. Many do not realize that there is an art to asking good questions until they read Chapter 25 "The Art (and Science) of Asking Questions." The vignette that begins this chapter demonstrates the difficulties that classroom teachers can sometimes face when they want to ask questions that will spark rich conversations about science concepts, but instead the questions result in limited or no discussion at all. This chapter provides the foundation for why developing good questioning skills is important to science teaching and learning, and sets the stage for what it can look like in a classroom. The research highlights the types of questions that work and don't work to promote students' scientific thinking. Building from the suggestions at the end of the chapter on how to become a better questioner, we use the methods class then to work through a series of activities in which the preservice teachers practice forming questions that serve various purposes and explore different scientific phenomena. They also learn to critique their own questioning skills and those of their peers through a mock interview workshop. As they move to teaching science in their early field experience, the preservice teachers are once again reminded at the end of the chapter of the tips for becoming a better questioner. They are challenged to select two or three skills that they want to work on over the five weeks during which they are teaching science to children in schools. After teaching, they reflect on how they perceive the use of those skills has helped them to build their knowledge and practice of becoming a better questioner and, thus, a better science teacher.

Conclusion

What we have shared are just two ways, albeit within different contexts, of how the chapters from this compendium can be used with teachers to support and further develop their understanding of how to teach science. Even though the chapters are grouped into topical themes, each has the potential to stand on its own and can provide teachers with a new perspective for thinking about their science teaching. We encourage all educators to think about how these articles can not only be used as an introduction to a topic but also as an anchor for discussions on effective, research-based elementary science practices.

General Teaching Goals

1

Helping Students Understand the Nature of Science

By Deborah L. Hanuscin and Eun J. Lee

"I keep coming across lessons and articles related to teaching students about the nature of science—what exactly does that mean? How can I help my students learn about the nature of science?"

What is meant by the "nature of science," and why is this important for students to learn?

Teachers help students develop process skills and inquiry abilities, as well as understand facts, concepts, and principles in science. A third goal of science teaching is helping students understand the "nature of science"—what science is and how science works. The nature of science addresses the importance of creativity and imagination in scientific work: how scientists invent explanations for phenomena; the difference between observation and inference; how scientific ideas are subject to change; and how culture and society influence science. The

National Science Education Standards (Content Standard G) emphasize that students should understand the power and limitations of science, the use of scientific knowledge in decision making, and science as an important part of culture (NRC 1996). By focusing on not only what we know but also how we know, teachers are providing students with a robust view of science.

What does the research say about students' ideas about the nature of science?

Students' ideas about science are informed by media images of science and scientists and are also affected by their school science experiences. Researchers have found that these experiences can result in the formation of myths and misconceptions about the nature of science. For example, Akerson and Abd-El-Khalick (2005) interviewed fourth-grade students who believed that their textbooks contain unchanging scientific truth and that science has little room for creativity because it is a straightforward procedure. Students also believed that science is based solely on what can be observed directly. Similarly, Driver and colleagues (1996) learned through interviews with nine-year-olds that students had difficulty differentiating between evidence and explanation, and failed to recognize the importance of inference to scientific work. Conley and colleagues (2004) asked fifth-grade students to respond to a series of questions about the source, certainty, development, and justification of scientific ideas. Students were likely to view the most important part of science as coming up with the "right" answer, and students thought scientists know everything about science already. Students' beliefs about science were not related to gender and ethnicity; however, low-achieving and low socioeconomic status students exhibited less sophisticated beliefs about the nature of science than their peers, which could be related to their opportunities to learn science.

What does research say about teaching the nature of science?

Teaching science by modeling how scientists do science is not enough. Researchers have shown that the nature of science must be a purposeful and explicit part of classroom lessons and discussions for students to develop their understanding. For example, Akerson and Abd-El-Khalick found that, despite immersion in inquiry-based instruction, fourth graders failed to develop an understanding of the tentative nature of science, instead claiming that the information in science textbooks is "not going to change because science doesn't change" (2005, p. 7). Khishfe and Abd-El-Khalick (2002) examined the development of sixth-grade students' understanding of the nature of science by comparing instruction in two cases: one in which the teacher introduced various ideas about the nature of science, then had students reflect on their ideas about science in the context of inquiry-based lessons, and one in which the nature of science was not an explicit part of classroom discussions. Students in the class where the nature of science was addressed explicitly demonstrated more substantial improvement in their understanding than the second group. Similarly, Akerson and Volrich (2006) found that when teachers emphasized the role of creativity in scientific work and the way in which scientific ideas are subject to change in light of new evidence, students improved their understanding. At the beginning of the study, the majority of Volrich's first graders believed that scientists do not change their ideas because once they figure out something, science is "done." In response to students' ideas, Volrich pointed out examples of how students changed their ideas during their investigations, and she concluded her lessons by raising the question, "How is what we did like what scientists do?" At the conclusion of her instruction, her students were able to explain that scientists can change their explanations and ideas because of new evidence.

How can I help my students learn about the nature of science?

As with any topic, to teach the nature of science, teachers must understand the content themselves, know what is important to teach, find out students' incoming ideas, and implement instructional activities and assessments to help students learn. *Science for All Americans* (AAAS 1990) can be a starting point for teachers to learn about the nature of science. Teachers can examine national and state standards to see what ideas about the nature of science are important to teach at their grade levels. Formative assessment probes (Keeley, Eberle, and Dorsey 2008) can help teachers diagnose students' incoming ideas about the nature of science, and example lessons (Bell 2008) can help teachers teach the nature of

science. Regardless of the curriculum, it is important to remember that every lesson portrays an image of science to students and conveys information about what science is and how science works. To make the nature of science an explicit part of instruction, ideas about science should be planned for, taught, and assessed intentionally. Teachers can

- invite students to express their own ideas about science and scientists through talking, writing, and drawing;

- help students critically evaluate popular images of science and scientists;

- introduce students to "behind the scenes" information about how the scientific ideas in their textbooks came about;

- encourage students to reflect on their ideas about the nature of science and how these ideas are illustrated by their own classroom science investigations; and

- invite students to consider specific ideas about the nature of science during instruction by asking questions such as, *What might cause scientists to change their ideas?* or *How do you think scientists determined what dinosaurs looked like if they only had the bones?*

References

Akerson, V. L., and F. Abd-El-Khalick. 2005. How should I know what scientists do—I'm just a kid: Fourth-grade students' conceptions of nature of science. *Journal of Elementary Science Education* 17: 1–11.

Akerson, V. L., and M. Volrich. 2006. Teaching nature of science explicitly in a first-grade internship setting. *Journal of Research in Science Teaching* 43 (4): 377–394.

American Association for the Advancement of Science (AAAS). 1990. *Science for all Americans.* New York: Oxford University Press.

Bell, R. L. 2008. *Teaching the nature of science through process skills: Activities for grades 3–8.* London: Allyn and Bacon.

Conley, A. M., P. R. Pintrich, I. Vekiri, and D. Harrison. 2004. Changes in epistemological beliefs in elementary science students. *Contemporary Educational Psychology* 29 (2): 186–204.

Driver, R., J. Leach, R. Millar, and P. Scott. 1996. *Young people's images of science.* Buckingham: Open University Press.

Keeley, P., F. Eberle, and C. Dorsey. 2008. *Uncovering student ideas in science, volume 3: Another 25 formative assessment probes.* Arlington, VA: NSTA Press.

Khishfe, R., and F. Abd-El-Khalick. 2002. Influence of explicit and reflective versus implicit inquiry-oriented instruction on sixth graders' views of nature of science. *Journal of Research in Science Teaching* 39 (7): 551–578.

National Research Council (NRC). 1996. *National science education standards.* Washington, DC: National Academies Press.

2

Learning to Observe and Infer

By Deborah L. Hanuscin and Meredith Park Rogers

"I have always thought that observation is the key to science but national and state standards say to emphasize inference and explanation. But shouldn't observation come first?"

How do scientists use observation and inference?

When exploring phenomena, scientists draw from many resources to gather information about what is happening and to develop explanations. Sometimes they gather evidence directly using their senses; other times, direct observation is not possible. For example, atoms are much too small to be seen, even with the most powerful microscopes. Yet Rutherford proposed a model of atomic structure based on his observation that alpha particles deflected at different angles when they tried to pass through a thin layer of gold foil. His direct observations alone could not fully explain what was occurring in this experiment

(Abd-El-Khalick 2002). Rutherford also inferred from his prior knowledge about charges and deflection to explain that there must be something massive and tiny, deep within each atom, interfering with the passing of the alpha particles—now known as the nucleus. In science, this process of logical reasoning is referred to as inference and allows scientists to use their observations to understand a phenomenon, even when they cannot directly observe it.

In what ways are observation and inference important in elementary classroom science?

Students need to develop these inquiry skills at an early age, so that, like scientists, they can use observation and inference to construct explanations for phenomena (Harlen 2001). When learning science, students cannot rely on observation alone. In elementary science students can observe many phenomena directly (e.g., an object floating or sinking) but not all. For example, when studying electrical circuits, students cannot see electrical current. Rather, they make inferences about the flow of current from their observations of the brightness of the bulb. As students add bulbs to a circuit in series, they observe the bulbs get dimmer but remain equally bright. From this they may infer that the current has lessened although each of the bulbs receives the same amount of current. Combining what they observed (lights equally dim) and inferred (current lessens but each bulb receives the same amount), students can generate an explanation for how resistance affects the flow of current in a circuit.

What difficulties do students encounter in understanding how scientists use observation and inference?

Research shows young learners often believe scientists use only observation when developing explanations, as they do not understand the importance of inference to scientific work. In a study of 23 fourth-grade students' views of science, researchers asked how scientists use observation and inference to learn about dinosaurs (Akerson and Abd-El-Khalick 2005). The research-

ers found most students believed scientists used evidence such as bones and fossils to explain what dinosaurs looked like. However, when asked to describe how scientists determine the color of dinosaurs, students gave a variety of responses or no response at all. Findings from this study demonstrate elementary students' difficulty in recognizing the role inference plays in helping scientists to understand natural phenomenon.

Similarly, when Akerson and Volrich (2006) asked first graders how scientists knew what dinosaurs looked like, many students believed scientists had actually seen whole dinosaurs, not that scientists inferred what dinosaurs looked like based on fossil evidence. After teaching students how to observe and infer by modeling those processes in her lessons and being explicit about the role of observation and inference in science, Volrich found that her students improved their understanding of the two processes and the importance of each to scientific work.

For example, after instruction, 12 of the 14 students discussed how scientists observed and compared bones to infer what dinosaurs looked like and how they lived. These students developed a better understanding of how scientists use both observations and inferences to explain science phe-nomena. These studies demonstrate that young children have the ability to learn the difference between observa-tion and inference and their role in science, but teachers must be explicit about the difference between the two and their role in the development of scientific knowledge.

How can I develop my elementary students' observation and inference skills?

Researchers describe the need for stu-dents to have multiple opportunities and social interaction to learn about the differences between observa-tion and inference and their role in developing scientific explanations (Harlen 2001; Simpson 2000). For example, Herrenkohl and Guerra's (1998) examination of fourth-grade students' science learning found an increase in student learning when (1) students had opportunities to discuss in small groups and as a class what they observed and inferred; (2) stu-dents saw the teacher modeling these scientific practices (i.e., observing and inferring); and (3) these practices became a part of the normative prac-tice of their science class regardless of the content. In addition, Metz (2000) found that elementary students' sci-

ence learning needs to be scaffolded around a metacognitive approach, in which students are asked to think about what they know (i.e., what they can directly observe) and what they do not directly know (i.e., what they need to infer).

Drawing from this research base, teachers can build a classroom environment in which students build their understanding, like scientists, through observing and inferring. The following instructional strategies are recommended:

- Giving students multiple opportunities to practice observing and discussing similarities and differences they find in their observations;

- Asking students challenging questions throughout their explorations to focus their attention on situations where it is possible and not possible to gather data using observations;

- Encouraging students to look for patterns and make generalizations from their data (i.e., inferences); and

- Establishing a positive learning environment where students feel comfortable challenging one another's claims about observations and inferences and how they were used to generate explanations.

Helping children develop their skills of observation and inference in science while emphasizing the importance of each skill will also help them develop a better understanding of how scientists generate knowledge about the world.

References

Abd-El-Khalick, F. 2002. Rutherford's enlarged: A content-embedded activity to teach about nature of science. *Physics Education* 37 (1): 64–68.

Akerson, V. L., and F. S. Abd-El-Khalick. 2005. How should I know what scientists do?—I am just a kid: Fourth-grade students' conceptions of nature of science. *Journal of Elementary Science Education* 17 (1): 1–11.

Akerson, V. L., and M. Volrich. 2006. Teaching nature of science explicitly in a first-grade internship setting. *Journal of Research in Science Teaching* 43 (4): 377–394.

Harlen, W. 2001. *Primary science…taking the plunge: How to teach primary science more effectively for ages 5 to 12.* Portsmouth, NH: Heinemann.

Herrenkohl, L. R., and M. R. Guerra. 1998. Participant structures, scientific discourse, and student engagement in fourth grade. *Cognition and Instruction* 16 (4): 431–473.

Metz, K. E. 2000. Young children's inquiry in biology: Building the knowledge bases to empower independent inquiry. In *Inquiring into inquiry learning and teaching in science,* eds., J. Minstrell and E. H. van Zee, 371–404. Washington, DC: AAAS.

Simpson, D. 2000. Collaborative conversations: Strategies for engaging students in productive dialogues. In *Inquiring into inquiry learning and teaching in science,* eds., J. Minstrell and E. H. van Zee, 176–183. Washington, DC: AAAS.

3

Explaining Science

By Mark J. Gagnon and Sandra K. Abell

"The National Science Education Standards state that there should be less emphasis on 'science as exploration and experimentation' and more emphasis on 'science as argument and explanation.' Can my students do this? Can I?"

What is explanation, and why is it important in science?

We often think of science as exploration and experiment. However, classrooms that portray only this view of science fail to capture an essential feature of science—evidence-based explanation. When scientists encounter patterns in the world, they construct theories to explain them. What does it mean to explain in science? Explanation is more than summarizing the data that have been collected. Explanations tell *why* phenomena occur. Explanations involve a leap of imagination; scientists explain by building and testing models of how the world works. Scientific explanations emphasize evidence and

employ accepted scientific principles. For example, different states of matter are explained by the arrangement and movement of molecules. The best explanations are the simplest and take into account the most evidence. The central role of explanation in science should be part of science classrooms. According to the National Academies Committee on Science Learning, Kindergarten through Eighth Grade (Duschl, Schweingruber, and Shouse 2007), elementary science should be aimed at helping students "know, use, and interpret scientific explanations … [and] generate and evaluate scientific evidence and explanations" (p. 36). But can elementary students generate viable explanations using scientific evidence?

Can children generate and evaluate explanations from evidence?

To what extent is it reasonable to ask elementary students to generate scientific explanations? Several educational psychologists have explored this question in clinical settings. Sodian, Zaitchik, and Carey (1991) presented first and second graders with two conflicting hypotheses and asked them to choose a test to decide between them. Seventy-five percent of the first graders and all of the second graders were able to choose a conclusive test. Samarapungavan (1992) interviewed first, third, and fifth graders to find out what criteria they used for choosing among alternate explanations about the relative shapes, positions, and movements of heavenly bodies. She found that even the youngest children could use logic to choose the best explanation based on evidence. Ruffman and colleagues (1993) used a set of interview tasks in the form of stories with four- to seven-year-olds to investigate how children understood the relation of evidence and explanation. They found that by age six, most children recognized how the characters in the stories might form correct or incorrect explanations based on the evidence. These studies demonstrate the potential of young children to think scientifically in psychology laboratories. However, how do students perform in classroom settings?

What do classrooms focused on explanation and evidence look like?

Several studies about students' ability to construct scientific explanations have taken place in elementary classrooms with classroom teachers as part of the research team. The researchers have found that students at various grade levels can be successful in generating scientific explanations from evidence. Kawasaki, Herrenkohl, and Yeary (2004) examined the evolution of students' explanation building and modeling in a unit on sinking and floating. They found that students initially did not offer explanations but merely described the phenomenon. With time and prompting by the teacher, students began to discuss relations among variables and eventually used model-based reasoning, where they realized that explanations might need to change in light of new evidence. In Taiwan, Wu and Hsieh (2006) studied how sixth graders constructed explanations about force and motion and electricity. Like Kawasaki and her colleagues, they found that, although at first students did not include data as evidence in their discussions or presentations, with more experience they were able to support their explanations with data. Abell and Roth (1995) found that fifth graders could generate their own models of energy flow from plants to herbivores to predators through an ecosystem that took into account evidence from their classroom terraria, but the students had difficulty understanding the standard scientific model of the energy pyramid. In a study of third graders' reasoning about principles of sound, Abell, Anderson, and Chezem (2000) found that students used evidence to support their explanations and to select among explanations. However, not all students ended the sound unit agreeing about how sound is produced. What these classroom-based studies tell us is that learning to generate and use scientific explanations is a reasonable expectation in elementary science classrooms, but it does not happen automatically without specific scaffolds provided by the teacher.

How can teachers build a classroom atmosphere for developing explanations?

We can learn ways to support students as they generate explanations in science by reading how other teachers have accomplished this in their classrooms. Karen Gallas (1995) conducted numerous "science talks" with first- through fourth-grade students. She described the anatomy of a science talk, including the role of the teacher in helping students uncover children's questions and explanations. Her examples are useful models. Folsom and her partners (2007) helped kindergartners develop evidence-based explanations about animals. They described specific techniques—asking students to write evidence-based explanations and defend them, probing students for evidence when they offer an explanation (What makes you think that?), asking guiding questions about how students might figure something out, and holding students "scientifically accountable" for their explanations (versus merely correcting their ideas). In the examples of classroom-based research presented in this chapter, the role of the teacher is clear. Teachers helped students compare and think through their developing explanations during scientist meetings, gave students opportunities to argue and explain their ideas, and listened to their explanations to understand their thinking. In classrooms where scientific explanations are the focus, the student becomes the center of sense-making while the teacher carefully structures and directs the work from the side.

References

Abell, S. K., G. Anderson, and J. Chezem. 2000. Science as argument and explanation: Inquiring into concepts of sound in third grade. In *Inquiring into inquiry learning and teaching in science,* eds. J. Minstrell and E. van Zee, 65–79. Washington, DC: American Association for the Advancement of Science.

Abell, S. K., and M. Roth. 1995. Reflections on a fifth-grade life science lesson: Making sense of children's understanding of scientific models. *International Journal of Science Education* 17 (1): 59–74.

Duschl, R. A., H. A. Schweingruber, and A. W. Shouse. 2007. *Taking science to school: Learning and teaching science in grades K–8.* Washington, DC: The National Academies Press.

Folsom, J., C. Hunt, M. Cavicchio, A. Schoenemann, and M. D'Amato. 2007. How do you know that? Guiding early elementary students to develop evidence-based explanations about animals. *Science and Children* 44 (5): 20–25.

Gallas, K. 1995. *Talking their way into science: Hearing children's questions and theories, responding with curricula.* New York: Teachers College Press.

Kawasaki, K., L. R. Herrenkohl, and S. A. Yeary. 2004. Theory building and modeling in a sinking and floating unit: A case study of third- and fourth-grade students' developing epistemologies of science. *International Journal of Science Education* 26 (11): 1299–1324.

Ruffman, T., J. Perner, D. R. Olson, and M. Doherty. 1993. Reflecting on scientific thinking: Children's understanding of the hypothesis-evidence relation. *Child Development* 64 (6): 1617–1636.

Samarapungavan, A. 1992. Children's judgments in theory choice tasks: Scientific rationality in childhood. *Cognition* 45 (1): 1–32.

Sodian, B., D. Zaitchik, and S. Carey. 1991. Young children's differentiation of hypothetical beliefs from evidence. *Child Development* 62(4): 753–766.

Wu, H-K., and C-E. Hsieh. 2006. Developing sixth graders' inquiry skills to construct explanations in inquiry-based learning environments. *International Journal of Science Education* 28 (11): 1289–1313.

4

Defending Inquiry

By Chris Ohana

"I am an elementary school teacher in Charlotte, North Carolina. I use hands-on inquiry lessons in science but my administrator and a few colleagues think it looks like "play time." What is the evidence for the use of inquiry in elementary science?"

What is inquiry?

The word *inquiry* has been tossed around so frequently that it has lost much meaning. Inquiry is somewhat elusive to define, but here we will defer to the National Science Education Standards (NSES): "Inquiry is a multifaceted activity that involves making observations; posing questions; examining books and other sources… planning investigations; using tools to gather, analyze and interpret data; proposing answers, explanations and predictions; and communicating the results." (NRC 1996, p. 23)

To be brief, inquiry is what scientists do; it's the development, exploration, and explanation of questions in a systematic way. It can come from a number of processes including careful observations, experiments, reading, or discussions and collaboration, and is essentially any honest way to collect evidence. Inquiry-based lessons incorporate each of the science processes where most appropriate. Science is taught through inquiry in order to learn how scientists work, improve problem-solving skills, and improve student learning of content. It is this last point we will explore.

What effect does inquiry have on learning?

Administrators, parents, and teachers are focused on what works. Their interest is largely on programs, strategies, and policies that improve student understanding of content. If we advocate for inquiry-based teaching, then we must be able to back it up. Fortunately, there has been much published that helps our case. Shymansky and his colleagues (1990) have shown positive effects of inquiry-based curricula on student achievement. EDC's Center for Science Education is conducting a project that will add a valuable synthesis of the existing research on inquiry and student achievement. Their report is available at *http://ltd. edc.org/resource-library/inquiry-based-science-instruction%E2%80%94what-it-and-does-it-matter*.

Does inquiry work with all student populations?

Teaching through inquiry methods has been shown to improve the understanding of science with students of poverty (Lynch et al. 2005) who qualify for special education (Scruggs and Mastropieri 1993) and with students who are English language learners (Lee et al. 2005). The work of Lee et al. (2005) has illustrated that the longer students are exposed to a high-quality, inquiry-based program, the higher their achievement.

What are the problems in teaching through inquiry?

Teaching for understanding through inquiry takes more time and resources than simply telling students what they should know or having them read a textbook. As a result, it is just impossible to "cover" the amount of material

that is found in most textbooks, and unfortunately, in most state standards. It takes courage to not take the time to mention everything that could be on the test, especially if your administrators insist that you "cover" all of the standards. But research does support the counterintuitive result that students who spend more time really learning a smaller, coherent amount of important content will perform as well or better on a comprehensive test than students who have been exposed to all of the content available to be put on the test.

What support, skills, and abilities do teachers need to teach through inquiry?

Teachers need to understand students, science content, and the pedagogical demands of inquiry teaching in order to be effective (Anderson 2002). Teachers who are expected to teach through inquiry must have solid backgrounds in science education as well as science content and the formative assessment skills to draw out and recognize their students' ideas and to guide them, through inquiry, toward scientific thinking.

Do these skills in science affect achievement in other areas?

When inquiry is structured well, it takes time, professional development, and administrative support. The rewards include higher achievement, improved attitudes in science, and improved higher-order thinking skills. While inquiry is not the only way to teach, it is an important foundation for science learning. We can't afford to not make the investment.

References

Anderson, R. 2002. Reforming science teaching: What research says about inquiry. *Journal of Science Teacher Education* 13 (1): 1–12.

Donovan, M. S., and J. D. Bransford. 2005. *How students learn: Science in the classroom.* Washington, DC: National Academies Press.

Lee, O., R. Deaktor, J. Hart, P. Cuevas, and C. Enders. 2005. An instructional intervention's impact on the science and literacy achievement of culturally and linguistically diverse elementary students. *Journal of Research in Science Teaching* 42 (8): 857–887.

Lynch, S., J. Kuipers, C. Pyke, and M. Szesze. 2005. Examining the effects of a highly rated science curriculum unit on diverse students: Results from a planning grant. *Journal on Research on Science Teaching* 42 (8): 912–946.

National Research Council (NRC). 1996. *National science education standards.* Washington, DC: National Academies Press.

Scruggs, T. E., and M. A. Mastropieri. 1993. Reading vs. doing: The relative effects of textbook-based and inquiry-oriented approaches to science learning in special education classrooms. *The Journal of Special Education* 27 (1): 1–15.

Shymansky, J. A., L. V. Hedges, and G. Woodworth. 1990. A reassessment of the effects of inquiry-based science curricula of the 60s on student performance. *Journal of Research on Science Teaching* 27 (2): 127–144.

Strategies to Facilitate Learning in Science

5

Examining the Learning Cycle

By Patrick L. Brown and Sandra K. Abell

"I use hands-on activities with my fifth graders as often as possible. But I worry that my students won't learn science just by doing activities. Is there a way to structure science lessons to go beyond the hands-on component?"

Is hands-on alone enough to learn science?

Jerome Bruner (1960) introduced the idea of "discovery learning," in which students interact with their environment to discover new ideas. However, teachers who have tried to help students "discover" science ideas by doing hands-on activities often are frustrated when students do not learn what the teachers expected. Why should we expect our students to "discover" ideas that took science hundreds of years to invent? Maybe something is missing from the discovery approach.

Kathy Roth (1989) compared different approaches to teaching science concepts like photosynthesis to fifth graders. She found that students understood the science concepts better when hands-on activities were followed by student discussion and writing and when the teacher introduced ideas that challenged student misconceptions. Magnusson and Palinscar (2005) described a fourth-grade science class in which students investigated light and then attempted to explain its properties through dialogue with the teacher. In each of these cases, hands-on was necessary but not sufficient to help students learn science. So how can teachers structure science lessons to go beyond a hands-on activity?

What is the learning cycle?

Roth, Driver, Magnusson, and Palinscar all employed a learning cycle approach to help students learn science. First fully described in 1967 by Karplus and Thier for the Science

Curriculum Improvement Study (SCIS), the learning cycle is based on three phases of instruction: (1) exploration, which provides students with firsthand experiences to investigate science phenomena; (2) concept introduction, which allows students to build science ideas through interaction with peers, texts, and teachers; and (3) concept application, which asks students to use these science ideas to solve new problems. This teaching and learning cycle alternates between hands-on and minds-on activities, both of which are necessary for learning science.

Why is a learning cycle needed?

Cognitive scientists tell us that students need to relate new ideas to their experience and place new ideas into a framework for understanding (Bransford, Brown, and Cocking 2001). Thus exploring phenomena before explaining them is critical for learning. Researchers have found that students benefit when all three phases of the learning cycle are present (Renner, Abraham, and Birnie 1988). Abraham and Renner (1986) investigated whether the three stages of the learning cycle are in their optimal sequence. Trying various sequences in several high school science classes, they found

that when concept introduction followed exploration, students learned better. The introduction of terms after investigations helps students connect new concepts with prior experiences. However, multiple experiences may be required. In a study of upper elementary students, Nuthall (1999) found that students needed three to four experiences with new science ideas before they were able to commit these ideas to long-term memory.

Since Karplus and Thier introduced the learning cycle, several variations have been invented. However, each new version retains the essence of the original learning cycle—exploration before concept introduction. One popular contemporary learning cycle is the BSCS 5E Instructional Model—Engage, Explore, Explain, Elaborate, Evaluate (Bybee 1997). It incorporates the three core learning cycle phases while adding Engage and Evaluate to facilitate what Roth (1989) would call conceptual change. The Engage phase of the 5E is designed to captivate student attention and uncover students' current knowledge. The Evaluate phase is a chance for the teacher to assess student progress and for students to reflect on their new understandings.

How does the learning cycle affect students?

Several studies have examined the learning that results from cyclic approaches to science instruction. Renner, Abraham, and Birnie (1988) found greater achievement and retention when concepts were introduced after experiences. Gerber, Cavallo, and Marek (2001) found that students taught via a learning cycle scored higher on a test of scientific reasoning. Beeth and Hewson (1999) studied one teacher's science instruction in grades 4–6. She alternated hands-on activities with goal-directed discussion; her students improved their science understanding as well as their engagement in scientific discourse. Thus, a learning cycle approach helps students make sense of scientific ideas, improve their scientific reasoning, and increase their engagement in science class.

What can teachers do to change to learning cycle instruction?

If your science curriculum is dominated by a textbook, the first step in developing a learning cycle approach is to put the activities first (exploration). When students read the chapter (concept introduction) after the activity, they will have an experience to which to link the chapter ideas. You can find many ideas for employing learning cycles to teach

particular science concepts in NSTA journals (for example, Cavallo 2001, 2005; McNall and Bell 2004). Once you have mastered designing a few lessons in which explanations follow explorations, you will be ready to invent learning cycles for all of your science units. Books like Abell and Volkmann (2006) demonstrate how learning cycles can work across the elementary grades and across the science curriculum.

References

Abell, S. K., and M. J. Volkmann. 2006. *Seamless assessment in science: A guide for elementary and middle school teachers.* Portsmouth, NH: Heinemann.

Abraham, M. R., and J. W. Renner. 1986. The sequence of learning cycle activities in high school chemistry. *Journal of Research in Science Teaching* 23 (2): 121–143.

Beeth, M. E., and P. W. Hewson. 1999. Learning goals in exemplary science teacher's practice: Cognitive and social factors in teaching for conceptual change. *Science Education* 83 (6): 738–760.

Bransford, J., A. Brown, and R. Cocking. 2001. *How people learn: Brain, mind, experience, and school.* Washington, DC: National Academies Press.

Bruner, J. 1960. *The process of education.* Cambridge, MA: Harvard University Press.

Bybee, R. W. 1997. *Achieving scientific literacy: From purposes to practices.* Portsmouth, NH: Heinemann.

Cavallo, A. 2001. Convection connections. *Science and Children* 38 (8): 20–25.

Cavallo, A. 2005. Cycling through plants. *Science and Children* 42 (7): 22–27.

Gerber, B. L., A. M. L. Cavallo, and E. A. Marek. 2001. Relationship among informal learning environments, teaching procedures, and scientific reasoning abilities. *International Journal of Science Education* 23 (5): 535–549.

Karplus, R., and H. D. Thier. 1967. *A new look at elementary school science.* Chicago: Rand McNally.

Magnusson, S. J., and A. S. Palinscar. 2005. Teaching to promote the development of scientific knowledge and reasoning about light at the elementary school level. In *How students learn: Science in the classroom,* eds. M. S. Donovan and J. D. Bransford, 421–474. Washington, DC: National Academies Press.

McNall, R. L., and R. L. Bell. 2004. Discovering flowers in a new light. *Science and Children* 41 (4): 36–39.

Nuthall, G. 1999. The way students learn: Acquiring knowledge from an integrated science and social studies unit. *The Elementary School Journal* 99 (4): 303–341.

Renner, J. W., M. R. Abraham, and H. H. Birnie. 1988. The necessity of each phase of the learning cycle in teaching high school physics. *Journal of Research in Science Teaching* 25 (1): 39–58.

Roth, K. J. 1989. Science education: It's not enough to "do" or "relate." *American Educator* 13 (4): 46–48.

6

Using Analogies in Elementary Science

By S. Rená Smith and Sandra K. Abell

"My colleague down the hall often uses analogies, such as 'an ecosystem is like a shopping mall,' in her science teaching. However, I've heard that analogies can sometimes reinforce misconceptions. Are there ways to use analogies effectively to help students learn science?"

Why should I use analogies in science class?

Using analogies in science classrooms helps students make connections between everyday life and the concepts we are trying to teach. Analogies help students form a bridge between their existing knowledge and new knowledge. Humans use analogical reasoning naturally, especially when trying to explain something to others. Throughout history, scientists' analogical reasoning has led to important scientific discoveries. (For example, the chemist August Kekulé envisioned a snake chasing its tail and recognized the ring structure of benzene.) In the science classroom, Glynn (2007) points out that many of our conversations start with "It's just like … ," "It's similar to … ," or "Think of it in this way… ." By using analogies, teachers can help students create mental models that link new (and sometimes abstract) ideas to prior experiences. For example, Chiu and Lin (2005) studied student learning of electricity in a fourth-grade class in Taiwan. They designed an experiment with four different instructional groups—one received no analogies in instruction, while three groups did. One analogy group learned a water flow analogy for electric circuits, while the other two groups learned additional analogies for electricity, such as the obstacle course, crowded people, and a marathon runner. The researchers found that using analogies promoted student understanding and helped them overcome their misconceptions. (You can find many examples of misconceptions in Driver et al. 1994.)

Are all analogies the same?

All analogies make a comparison between a target concept (the concept you are aiming to have students understand) and the analog concept. The most effective analogs are more familiar to learners than the target concepts yet share certain features. Analogies can be spontaneous or formal. Spontaneous metaphors are generated during the course of a lesson. Formal analogies are planned by teachers or presented in curriculum materials. Although analogies have been shown to help students learn science (Treagust 2007), most textbooks ignore their power. In a study of 80 elementary science textbooks, Newton (2003) found that 45 contained no analogies at all. Of the texts that did contain analogies, the average was 2.6 per book. These analogies could be classified as structural or functional. Structural analogies focus on similarities in appearance or structure between the target concept and analog concept; for example, "the Earth is like an orange." Functional analogies link to a behavior, or explain how something operates—"a cell is like a refrigerator." Students can generate analogies quite readily. May, Hammer,

and Roy (2006) found third graders spontaneously made analogies during a unit about earthquakes. The researchers demonstrated how one student, through defending his analogy, was able to think more deeply about and revise his explanations.

Is there a "right" way to use analogies with my students?

Researchers have proposed several models for teaching science with analogies. For example, Glynn's (1996, 2007) Teaching-With-Analogies (TWA) model helps teachers use analogies systematically and effectively. First, the teacher introduces the target scientific concept, such as the cell. Second, the teacher asks students to think about what they know about an analog concept, perhaps the Lego. Next, the teacher guides students to identify important features of cells and Legos and to map their similarities and differences. For example, both individual cells and Legos can be built into something larger, but cells have a number of different components (the organelles) and Legos are uniform. Finally, students draw conclusions about the cell.

Treagust, Harrison, and Venville (1998) worked with a group of teachers who modified the TWA model to be more user-friendly in their classrooms.

Their model, called FAR (Focus, Action, and Reflection), offers guidelines for thinking about the target, the analog, and the students during each phase of instruction. Focus occurs at the start of the lesson, in which the teacher analyzes the difficulty of the target concept, what students already know about the concept, and their degree of familiarity with the analog. For example, the teacher would think about difficulties students might have understanding cells and how the Legos analogy might help. During the Action phase, teachers help students discuss the features of the target and analog, analyzing their similarities and differences. After the lesson is Reflection, in which teachers consider how the analogy helped students learn and consider next steps in instruction. After implementing lessons using the FAR guidelines, teachers reported increased confidence and enthusiasm in teaching the concept and an increased awareness of the need to establish student familiarity with the analog and help them analyze similarities and differences.

How can I get started?

Jakobson and Wickman (2007) studied children's use of analogies in seven elementary classrooms (grades 1–4) in Sweden while observing units about properties of matter, electricity, buds, shadows, and soil. They found that students frequently generated analogies in class to make sense of what they observed. These metaphors helped students use everyday ideas to contend with scientific language. Teachers could begin by listening to students and recognizing their spontaneous metaphors. However, generating analogies without analysis can lead to misunderstandings. Thus teachers also need to help students think about where the analogy works and where it breaks down in making sense of the target. For example, in comparing an ecosystem to a shopping mall, students need to recognize that the energy transformations in an ecosystem do not correspond to the money exchanges in a shopping mall. In addition to listening to students, teachers can generate useful analogies of their own prior to a unit. Thinking about analogs that are familiar to most students is a good place to start. George de Mestral invented Velcro after returning from a hunting trip and noticing the burrs sticking to his clothes and his dog's fur. Similarly, students need to feel connected to the analogy, if it is to be useful in their learning. After generating analogies, teachers can use the TWA or FAR instructional models to help students learn. Analogies can become the Velcro that allows new information to be attached to students' prior knowledge, thus helping them make sense of scientific ideas.

References

Chiu, M. H., and J. W. Lin. 2005. Promoting fourth graders' conceptual change of their understanding of electric current via multiple analogies. *Journal of Research in Science Teaching* 42 (4): 429–464.

Driver, R., A. Squires, P. Rushworth, and V. Wood-Robinson. 1994. *Making sense of secondary science*. London: Routledge.

Glynn, S. 1996. Teaching with analogies: Building on the science textbook. *The Reading Teacher* 49 (6): 490–491.

Glynn, S. M. 2007. The teaching-with-analogies model. *Science and Children* 44 (8): 52–55.

Jakobson, B., and P. O. Wickman. 2007. Transformation through language use: Children's spontaneous metaphors in elementary school science. *Science Education* 16 (3): 267–289.

May, D. B., D. Hammer, and P. Roy. 2006. Children's analogical reasoning in a third-grade science discussion. *Science Education* 90 (2): 316–330.

Newton, L. D. 2003. The occurrence of analogies in elementary school science books. *Instructional Science* 31 (6): 353–375.

Treagust, D. F. 2007. General instructional methods and strategies. In *Handbook of Research on Science Education*, eds. S. K. Abell and N. G. Lederman, pp. 379–382. Mahwah, NJ: Lawrence Erlbaum Associates.

Treagust, D. F., A. G. Harrison, and G. J. Venville. 1998. Teaching science effectively with analogies: An approach for preservice and inservice teacher education. *Journal of Science Teacher Education* 9 (2): 85–101.

7

Making Time for Science Talk

By Mark J. Gagnon and Sandra K. Abell

"A friend of mine who teaches fifth grade claims that discussion in science is key for her students' learning. I've tried discussion with my third graders, but it takes up a lot of time, and I don't think they get that much out of reporting what they found to each other. Am I missing something about the role of talking in science class?"

Do elementary students benefit from classroom talk?

Cognitive scientists (Donovan and Bransford 2005) conclude that when teachers "simply give students the knowledge to incorporate, the practice and skill development of doing one's own mental search is shortchanged" (p. 579), but when students engage in classroom talk, they "become better at monitoring and questioning their own thinking" (p. 577). Science education researchers claim that elementary students have the ability to use science talk to explain, clarify, and justify what they have learned. In a study of

British 10- and 11-year-olds, Sorsby (1999) found that students used the strategies of clarifying, reconciling, and persuading others during discussions. Furthermore, students use their everyday language to help them reason and make sense of science. In a study of a sixth-grade urban, multi-age, bilingual classroom, Warren et al. (2001) described how the "science circle" was structured to allow students to ask questions, challenge each other, ask for clarification, tell stories, and even joke. The students' everyday language was a deep intellectual resource that helped them to argue, categorize, organize, and theorize about science phenomena. However, not all classroom science talk leads to such results.

What kind of "talk" are we talking about?

Researchers who study science talk find that most classroom discussions limit students' opportunities for sense making. Carlsen (1992) found that the structure of classroom science talk commonly followed "sequences of Initiation (usually a teacher question), Response (usually a student answer), and Evaluation (explicit feedback concerning the student's answer)" (p. 17). Lemke (1990) called this pattern Triadic Dialogue and asserted that this typical classroom structure is used to maintain control, not to help students generate science understanding. This "authoritative" approach (Mortimer 1998) encourages students to guess what the teacher is thinking, not to think on their own. Yet science discussions, if enacted differently, can help students learn science. Wertsch and Toma (1995) analyzed the kinds of talk in a Japanese fifth-grade classroom. They found that some talk served the authoritative function of conveying information, while "dialogic" talk helped students to generate meaning.

How can dialogue help students think about science?

According to Lemke (1990), "True Dialogue occurs when teachers ask questions to which they do not presume to already know the 'correct answer'" (p. 55). In dialogic science discussions, the students generate meaning from the classroom talk, rather than merely recite or report. Dialogic discussion is characterized by student spontaneity—comparing, expanding, and revising the ideas of others, and offering tentative explanations. Gallas (1995) found that her first and second graders could propose, support, expand, and revise their science theories, and in doing so, generate new meanings. Gee (1997) described types of sense-making discussion found in a second-grade classroom where students designed and carried out investigations about plants. For example, in "Design and Discovery Debate" students discussed the success of the components of their investigations. In "Anomaly Talk," students recognized unexpected outcomes. "Explaining Talk," the deepest kind of sense-making discussion, occurred when students interpreted their data through dialogue with each other. Such dialogue can occur when teachers make time and space for it, in the form of "science talks" (Gallas 1995), "scientists meetings" (Reardon 1993), or "science circles" (Warren et al. 2001).

How can teachers structure and facilitate scientific discussions?

Elementary classroom teacher researchers Karen Gallas (1995) and Jean Reardon (1993) found that classroom science talk is a rich source

of student thinking. Yet guiding dialogic discussions can be challenging
for teachers. Here are some helpful
strategies to get started on creating a
classroom where science talk is valued
and practiced (see also Gibbons 2002):

- Hold discussions following a
  shared science exploration.

- Ask open-ended questions that
  require thoughtful discussion.

- Give students time to think about
  a topic by assigning a discussion
  topic for after recess or the next
  day.

- Provide discussion rules,
  including directions on how to
  listen.

- Ask students to discuss their
  ideas in teams before opening
  discussion to the entire class.

- Structure discussions so that all
  students have the opportunity to
  participate.

- Provide scaffolding for student
  talk by asking for clarification,
  probing for more information,
  and modeling science talk for the
  speaker.

- Instead of playing the role
  of evaluator after student
  responses, listen and wait for
  other students to respond.

References

Carlsen, W. S. 1992. Closing down the
conversation: Discouraging student talk
on unfamiliar science content. *Journal
of Classroom Interaction* 27 (2): 15–21.

Donovan, M. S., and J. D. Bransford. 2005.
*How students learn: Science in the
classroom.* Washington, DC: National
Academies Press.

Gallas, K. 1995. *Talking their way into
science.* New York: Teachers College
Press.

Gee, J. P. 1997. Science talk: Language
and knowledge in classroom
discussion. Paper presented at the
National Association for Research in
Science Teaching, Chicago, IL.

Gibbons, P. 2002. *Scaffolding language,
scaffolding learning: Teaching
second language learners in the
mainstream classroom.* Portsmouth,
NH: Heinemann.

Lemke, J. 1990. *Talking science:
Language, learning, and values.*
Norwood, NJ: Ablex.

Mortimer, E. F. 1998. Multivoicedness and
univocality in classroom discourse:
An example from theory of matter.
*International Journal of Science
Education* 20 (1): 67–82.

Reardon, J. 1993. Developing a
community of scientists. *In Science
workshop: A whole language
approach,* ed. W. Saul, 631–645.
Portsmouth, NH: Heinemann.

Sorsby, B. 1999. The child's world and the scientist's world: Can argumentation help to bridge the culture gap? Paper presented at the Fifth International History, Philosophy, and Science Teaching Conference. Como, Italy.

Warren, B., C. Ballenger, M. Ogonowski, A. S. Rosebery, and J. Hudicourt-Barnes. 2001. Rethinking diversity in learning science: The logic of everyday sense-making. *Journal of Research in Science Teaching* 38 (5): 529–552.

Wertsch, J. V., and C. Toma. 1995. Discourse and learning in a classroom: A sociocultural approach. In *Constructivism in education,* eds. L. P. Steffe, and J. Gale, 159–174. Hillsdale, NJ: Lawrence Erlbaum Associates.

8

Project-Based Science

By Patrick L. Brown and Sandra K. Abell

"I want my fifth graders to tackle bigger science projects that are driven by meaningful and relevant questions. Is project-based science the way to go?"

What are the key features of project-based science?

Project-based science offers a way for teachers to design long-term units in which students plan and carry out personally relevant investigations. According to Krajcik and his colleagues, project-based science is defined by the following characteristics: (1) a driving question that engages students in investigating an authentic problem; (2) collaborative learning around the problem; (3) technology appropriate to the problem; and (4) products—called artifacts—that represent what students have learned (Krajcik et al. 1994). A worthwhile driving question creates a meaningful context and addresses rich science content; the driving question provides many opportunities for students to generate smaller investigative questions (Krajcik, Czerniak, and Berger 2002). The investigative questions allow students to design experiments and collect data that will extend their thinking about the driving question. For example, an elementary teacher might begin a unit on water pollution with a driving question such as, Is the tap water in our school safe to drink? The driving question motivates students to investigate characteristics of water such as pH or the presence of various chemicals, compare water from different sources, or understand national standards governing water quality. The essence of project-based science is that it situates science learning in relevant and meaningful aspects of a child's life. Therefore, the driving question is central to the lesson.

How can a question drive project-based science?

Using a driving question creates the context for further investigations. The results of these investigations in turn help students answer the driving question. For example, sixth-grade students in an urban school in Michigan investigated mechanical advantage starting with the driving question, How do machines help me build big things? The researchers reported significant gains in students' abilities to create hypotheses, identify variables, analyze data, and make scientific claims based on evidence as a result of the project-based unit (Rivet and Krajcik 2004). Gallagher et al. (1995) studied fifth graders in a unit about chemical interactions in ecosystems driven by the context of an accident scene where an overturned truck leaked corrosive materials. With supervision, students generated their own investigative questions and designed experiments to test how cars drove on roads where different strengths of hydrochloric acid had been applied. In these cases, the driving question led students into rich and meaningful investigations.

What are the benefits of project-based science?

Student engagement can be sustained throughout a problem-based unit, which can improve student content knowledge and motivation. In the study by Rivet and Krajcik mentioned previously, sixth-grade students took a walking tour around a construction site and then collaborated to design an everyday machine and modify it to increase its mechanical advantage. The researchers reported significant improvements in students' understanding of science content (balanced and unbalanced forces, simple and complex machines, and mechanical advantage), their ability to draw relationships among science concepts, and their inquiry skills. In Germany, Zumbach, Kumpf, and Koch (2004) compared two fourth-grade classrooms: a project-based science class and a traditional, teacher-directed class. Students were challenged to identify a small animal and decide what to do when encountering it in the woods. Students in the project-based science class had higher motivation and spent significantly more time out of class working on the project. Similar results were reported by Veermans and Jarvela (2004) who compared 10-year-old Finnish students involved in a four-week project investigating how different mammals adapt to their environments. Students in the project-based class had higher motivation, were more focused on learning the topic, and collaborated with peers to ask questions and form scientific explanations in answer to the driving question. In the United States, Lee et al. (2005) researched third- and fourth-grade students' performance during two project-based science units: one exploring measurement and matter and the other exploring the water cycle and weather. Within each unit, the lessons progressed from teacher-structured activities to student-directed investigations. The researchers reported that students in both grade levels showed significant improvements on all measures of science achievement, including content knowledge and inquiry skills.

What are the challenges of project-based science?

Designing classroom activities and helping students ask investigative questions organized around a driving question can be challenging aspects of using a project-based science approach. Sage (1996) reported that third- and fourth-grade teachers had difficulties structuring a unit on plant needs around a driving question situated in the context of garden plants losing leaves and drooping. Teachers needed to learn how to guide students to generate investigative questions that moved them toward deeper levels

of thinking and understanding. Veermans and Jarvela (2004) found that project-based science presented social and emotional challenges for some students. Teachers needed to help students set goals and monitor their performance in achieving those goals throughout the project-based unit.

Project-based science also creates the need for methods of assessment that move beyond traditional paper-and-pencil tests. Teachers can provide formative feedback to students at different points in the project to help students monitor their own progress. Furthermore, project artifacts—like posters, presentations, and reports—can serve as summative evaluations of student learning (Marx et al. 1997). In their book on project-based science, Krajcik, Czerniak, and Berger (2002) give examples of the kinds of artifacts that students might create. For instance, students can create posters addressing why pumpkins decay after Halloween; use models to explain how ramps help move heavy objects; or create images using temperature probes and software tools to see who has the warmest hands in class. While project-based science presents some challenges for students and teachers, its advantage is making science learning opportunities motivating and meaningful.

References

Gallagher, S. A., W. J. Stepien, B. J. Sher, and D. Workman. 1995. Implementing problem-based learning in science classrooms. *School Science and Mathematics* 95 (3): 136–146.

Krajcik, J., P. Blumenfeld, R. Marx, and E. Solloway. 1994. A collaborative model for helping middle grade teachers learn project-based instruction. *The Elementary Science Journal* 94 (5): 483–498.

Krajcik, J. S., C. M. Czerniak, and C. F. Berger. 2002. *Teaching science in elementary and middle school classrooms: A project-based approach.* New York: McGraw Hill.

Lee, O., R. A. Deaktor, J. E. Hart, P. Cuevas, and C. Enders. 2005. An instructional intervention's impact on the science and literacy achievement of culturally and linguistically diverse elementary students. *Journal of Research in Science Teaching* 42(8): 857–887.

Marx, R. W., P. C. Blumenfeld, J. S. Krajcik, and E. Soloway. 1997. Enacting project-based science: Challenges for practice and policy. *Elementary School Journal* 97 (4): 341–358.

Rivet, A. E., and J. S. Krajcik. 2004. Achieving standards in urban systemic reform: An example of a sixth grade project-based science curriculum. *Journal of Research in Science Teaching* 41 (7): 669–692.

Sage, S. M. 1996. *A qualitative examination of problem-based learning at the K–8 level: Preliminary findings.* Paper presented at the Annual Meeting of the American Educational Research Association, New York. (ED 398 263).

Veermans, M., and S. Jarvela. 2004. Generalized achievement goals and situational coping in inquiry learning. *Instructional Science* 32 (4): 269–291.

Zumbach, J., D. Kumpf, and S. C. Koch. 2004. Using multimedia to enhance problem-based learning in elementary school. *Information Technology in Childhood Education Annual* 25–37.

Teaching Science and Other Disciplines Together

9

Connecting With Other Disciplines

By Meredith Park Rogers and Sandra K. Abell

"I never seem to be able to cover everything in my curriculum. With the recent focus on assessing student achievement in literacy and math, I find little opportunity to teach anything else. How can I possibly prepare students for those tests and still help them make meaningful curricular connections to science?"

How can interdisciplinary instruction help students learn all subjects better?

Interdisciplinary instruction is a way of approaching curriculum by organizing content and processes from more than one discipline around a central theme, issue, problem, topic, or experience (Jacobs 1989). The National Science Education Standards (NRC 1996) call for interdisciplinary instruction to strengthen student science learning. Researchers have found that reading and writing instruction can connect to science through the reciprocal use of process skills, such as observing, comparing and contrasting, inferring,

explaining with evidence, and communicating (Baker and Saul 1994; Casteel and Isom 1994; Glynn and Muth 1994). Other researchers describe connections between science and mathematics that include using mathematical representations and developing problem-solving skills within the context of science (Frykholm and Glasson 2005; Lehman 1994). By weaving big ideas and important skills from different disciplines, teachers can maximize classroom time and reinforce concepts and skills across subjects.

How do students learn in interdisciplinary settings?

Instructional approaches that integrate curriculum have gained support from the field of cognitive science, in which researchers suggest that learning big ideas and frameworks is more powerful than learning individual or fragmented ideas (Caine and Caine 1993; Donovan and Bransford 2005). Interdisciplinary instruction encourages connections among disciplines to help learners construct stronger knowledge schema. Nuthall (1999) studied British elementary students' learning in an integrated science and social studies unit on Antarctica. He found compelling evidence to support an interdisciplinary approach. Because students could approach the content from different angles based on their interests, involvement, and background knowledge, there were greater opportunities to learn. The knowledge that the 12-year-olds built while learning about Antarctica across several disciplines affected the ways they organized new experiences and transformed them into new knowledge. For example, giving students opportunities to learn about Antarctica in both science and social studies contexts allowed for students' individual differences to be addressed and increased the chance that the students would make some connection to their background knowledge. When students had multiple ways to encounter and represent knowledge, their network of associations were more complex. Evidence from this study suggests that linking science and reading, writing, social studies, and mathematics through common themes or topics creates the potential for more effective learning.

What are cautions about using an interdisciplinary approach?

For all the potential benefits, an interdisciplinary approach also generates concerns. The first concern is that blurring disciplinary boundaries devalues the content of each discipline and student learning becomes superficial (Beane 1995; Dickinson and Young 1998). Roth (1994) expressed the concern that, in elementary classrooms where thematic interdisciplinary approaches are used, the science instruction that occurs may do more harm than good. In particular, "the content of theme units often [does] not focus on the powerful ideas or organizing concepts from the disciplines" (p. 44). When teachers create interdisciplinary units around themes such as teddy bears or apples, the curricular connections may be forced and important science concepts underemphasized.

The second concern is that an interdisciplinary approach may benefit one discipline more than another. Nixon and Akerson (2004) studied fifth graders who learned science integrated with reading and writing. Science and reading were successfully integrated in this classroom. However, the focus on science content hindered students' development of various writing skills. Nixon and Akerson suggested using science as a bridge for reading and writing when "the writing structure is familiar to the students and is being used to explore new science content, [or] the writing structure is open-ended so the students are not confined to a specific pattern, [and] when reading for information is connected to students' own questions" (p. 214).

How can teachers use science to develop meaningful interdisciplinary connections?

Park Rogers (2006) studied a team of four second-grade teachers who used science as the basis of their interdisciplinary curriculum. She found that they meaningfully integrated science, literacy, and mathematics in three ways: (1) by emphasizing process skills across subject areas, (2) by valuing inquiry as a common tool for learning, and (3) by employing a learning cycle model of instruction in all disciplines.

Teachers can start the process of designing interdisciplinary units by examining the standards in different curricular areas and finding commonalities. One place to start is with the National Science Education Standards (NRC 1996) unifying themes. The unifying themes (e.g., systems, change, models), as well as connected tools (e.g., measurement, representations), and shared processes (e.g., observing, predicting) are places for making meaningful curricular connections across disciplines.

Next, teachers can design interdisciplinary contexts in which students can achieve the standards. For example, investigations of local issues can engage students in thinking about science and social science concepts and help develop their understanding of probability and data analysis, which are parts of the mathematics standards. Asking students to examine representations of the Moon in various picture books can help them develop a critical stance toward reading and hone their concept of phases of the Moon (Abell, George, and Martini 2002). Using learning cycles to teach other subjects can promote inquiry throughout the curriculum. In these ways, teachers can find more time for science and maximize the connections that students make in their learning.

References

Abell, S. K., M. D. George, and M. Martini. 2002. The moon investigation: Instructional strategies for elementary science methods. *Journal of Science Teacher Education* 13 (2): 85–100.

Baker, L., and W. Saul. 1994. Considering science and language arts connections: A study of teacher cognition. *Journal of Research in Science Teaching* 31 (9): 1023–1037.

Beane, J. A. 1995. *Toward a coherent curriculum*. Alexandria, VA: Association for Supervision and Curriculum Development.

Caine, R. N., and G. Caine. 1993. Understanding a brain-based approach to learning and teaching, In *Integrating the curricula: A collection,* ed. R. Fogarty, 9–20. Arlington Heights, IL: IRI/Skylight Training and Publishing.

Casteel, C. P., and B. A. Isom. 1994. Reciprocal processes in science and literacy learning. *The Reading Teacher* 47 (7): 538–545.

Dickinson, V. L., and T. A. Young. 1998. Elementary science and language arts: Should we blur the boundaries? *School Science and Mathematics* 98 (6): 334–339.

Donovan, M. S., and J. D. Bransford. 2005. *How students learn: History, mathematics, and science in the classroom.* Washington, DC: National Academies Press.

Frykholm, J., and G. Glasson. 2005. Connecting science and mathematics instruction: Pedagogical context knowledge for teachers. *School Science and Mathematics* 105 (3): 127–141.

Glynn, S. M., and K. D. Muth. 1994. Reading and writing to learn science: Achieving scientific literacy. *Journal of Research in Science Teaching* 31 (9): 1057–1073.

Jacobs, H. 1989. *Interdisciplinary curriculum: Design and implementation.* Alexandria, VA: Association for Supervision and Curriculum Development.

Lehman, J. R. 1994. Integrating science and mathematics: Perceptions of preservice and practicing elementary teachers. *School Science and Mathematics* 94 (2): 58–64.

National Research Council (NRC). 1996. *National science education standards.* Washington, DC: National Academies Press.

Nixon, D., and V. L. Akerson. 2004. Building bridges: Using science as a tool to teach reading and writing. *Educational Action Research* 12 (2): 197–217.

Nuthall, G. 1999. The way students learn: Acquiring knowledge from an integrated science and social studies unit. *The Elementary School Journal* 99 (4): 303–341.

Park Rogers, M. 2006. Achieving a coherent curriculum in second grade: Science as the organizer. Unpublished PhD diss., University of Missouri–Columbia.

Roth, K. 1994. Second thoughts about interdisciplinary studies. *American Educator* 18 (1): 44–48.

10

Science and Mathematics: A Natural Connection

By Meredith Park Rogers, Mark J. Volkmann, and Sandra K. Abell

"I keep receiving flyers about professional development workshops that promote the integration of science and mathematics. Is this another trend that will soon go away, or is this something I should consider?"

Why should I integrate science and mathematics?

Nowhere in our daily lives do we separate tasks into specific subjects before we take action. Yet in schools we continue to teach the various disciplines as separate areas of knowledge. What if school, like the real world, could be more connected? Connections between science and mathematics seem natural. First, we use mathematics in science to organize and analyze data in tables and graphs. Mathematics helps us see and make sense of patterns in the data. Second, mathematics can help us represent scientific phenomena and understand scientific concepts. For example, we can use a mathematical formula to signify the relationship of mass and volume in the property of matter called density, or a graph to represent the amount of rain over one month. Student learning should benefit when teachers make the connections between science and mathematics explicit, because science provides concrete examples of abstract mathematical ideas, and mathematics helps students achieve deep understanding of science concepts (McBride and Silverman 1991). How can teachers capitalize on the natural connections between science and mathematics?

How can science and mathematics connections support student learning?

In both science and mathematics, we ask students to represent data and ideas in various ways. Research in mathematics education tells us that student understanding is built when teachers use multiple representations (e.g., pictures, written descriptions, tables, graphs, equations) to teach complex ideas. For example, Suh and Moyer (2007) found that when third graders used a variety of representations, their ability to think algebraically improved. Prain and Waldrip (2006) investigated the use of representations to teach elementary science. They learned that fourth through sixth graders who used a variety of representations demonstrated better conceptual understandings than students who lacked this knowledge. Teaching distinct types of representations and helping students translate among different representations aid student understanding (Lesh, Landau, and Hamilton 1983). Think of a class of second graders studying plant growth. They start by representing amount of growth with paper strips cut to the height of the plant. After collecting a series of data, the students paste their strips in sequence and create a bar graph representing growth. Through analyzing the various graphs, students see patterns in plant growth over time. Giving students opportunities to use representations and challenging them to explain phenomena in terms of different representations can lead to deeper learning of scientific and mathematical concepts.

What outcomes can I expect when I integrate science and mathematics?

Most data about the effect of integrating science and mathematics on student learning have come from testimonials of classroom teachers, not from data collected directly from students about their learning (Czerniak et al. 1999). For example, in a study of a thematic approach used in Alaskan K–8 classrooms, teachers reported that their students were more excited about learning and began to make connections across math and science concepts on their own (Peters, Schubeck, and Hopkins 1995). Greene (1991), who studied the implementation of the Mid-California Science Improvement Program (MCSIP), discussed the effect of integrating science and mathematics. She described a classroom of first graders studying various aspects of building while watching the construction of their new school. During their yearlong study, students explored using different kinds of materials (e.g., blocks, Tinker Toys, toothpicks) to construct different building designs. Through their exploration, the first graders learned about the physical properties (science) and geometrical properties (mathematics) of different materials. After one year of participating in MCSIP, student interest in both science and mathematics increased. Furthermore, 78% of students improved their scores on the National Assessment of Educational Progress (NAEP), exceeding nationwide scores for the area of Process of Inquiry. Results such as these demonstrate the effect of integrating science and mathematics on student learning, even in the early grades.

How can I begin to integrate science and mathematics?

Lonning and DeFranco (1997) proposed a continuum of integration for science and mathematics. The far ends of the continuum indicate independent mathematics or science (no integration), the middle is balanced mathematics and science (full integration), and between the ends and the middle is some integration with either a mathematics or science focus. When planning your integrated curriculum, first decide where on this continuum you want to be. Next, according to these researchers, you should ask two questions: What are the major mathematics and science concepts being taught in the activity? and Are these concepts worthwhile? That is, are they key elements in the curricula and meaningful to students? (p.

214). These questions logically lead to examining grade-level standards at the national, state, or local level.

You can also search for curriculum materials that are marketed as integrating science and mathematics. However, the integration these curricula promote often is based on common process skills such as observing, classifying, and analyzing (Roebuck and Warden 1998)—not on key concepts. Finally, it may be helpful to learn from those who have attempted integration in their classrooms. Goldston (2004) compiled a collection of reprints from *Science and Children* that focus on integrating basic process skills common to inquiry-based science and problem-based mathematics. Lehrer and Schauble (2002) tell stories about elementary teachers' firsthand experiences with integrating science and mathematics. Their stories describe how teachers can help students consider what is quality data to collect, how to represent the data, and how to use patterns within the data to formulate explanations. These classroom-tested lessons make a strong argument for authentic investigations that help students learn important skills and knowledge in both science and mathematics.

References

Czerniak, C. M., W. B. Weber, A. Sandmann, and J. Ahern. 1999. A literature review of science and mathematics integration. *School Science and Mathematics* 99 (8): 421–430.

Goldston, M. J. 2004. *Stepping up to science and math: Exploring the natural connections*. Arlington, VA: NSTA Press.

Greene, L. C. 1991. Science-centered curriculum in elementary school. *Educational Leadership* 49 (2): 42–46.

Lehrer, R., and L. Schauble. 2002. *Investigating real data in the classroom: Expanding children's understanding of math and science.* New York: Teachers College Press.

Lesh, R., M. Landau, and E. Hamilton. 1983. Conceptual models in applied mathematical problem solving research. In *Acquisition of mathematics concepts and processes*, eds. R. Lesh and M. Landau, 263–343. New York: Academic Press.

Lonning, R. A., and T. C. DeFranco. 1997. Integration of science and mathematics: A theoretical model. *School Science and Mathematics* 97 (4): 212–215.

McBride, J. W., and F. L. Silverman. 1991. Integrating elementary/middle school science and mathematics. *School Science and Mathematics* 91 (7): 285–292.

Peters, T., K. Schubeck, and K. Hopkins. 1995. A thematic approach: Theory and practice at the Aleknagik school. *Phi Delta Kappan* 76 (8): 633–636.

Prain, V., and B. Waldrip. 2006. An exploratory study of teachers' and students' use of multi-modal representations of concepts in primary science. *International Journal of Science Education* 28 (15): 1843–1866.

Roebuck, K. I., and M. A. Warden. 1998. Searching for the center on the mathematics-science continuum. *School Science and Mathematics* 98 (6): 328–333.

Suh, J., and P. S. Moyer. 2007. Developing students' representational fluency using virtual and physical algebra balances. *Journal of Computers in Mathematics and Science Teaching* 26 (2): 155–173.

11

Reading and Science

By Sandra K. Abell

"My students often choose science books at the library, but we have little time for reading any more than the textbook in science class. How can I help my students to get the most out of their science reading?"

Is there a place for science in reading (and vice versa)?

To become good readers, students need experience in reading for information. Science class is an ideal place for students to develop motivation and strategies for informational reading. Yet with the promotion of hands-on science, many teachers get the message that reading may be inappropriate in science. Nothing could be farther from the truth. Language is at the heart of science. According to Norris and Phillips (2003), science could not exist without a written language to record and disseminate ideas in ways that to allow them to be tested, elaborated, and sometimes refuted. While language-based activities such

as talking are considered critical in science learning (Gagnon and Abell 2007), the place of reading in science has been far less explored.

How can science support reading development?

When students are motivated to read, they read more. When students read more, they become better readers. In other words, motivation to read predicts reading achievement. Guthrie and his colleagues (2006) set out to test this idea in a third-grade science setting. They examined student outcomes in reading for classrooms with a high number of hands-on science activities compared to classrooms with few such activities and found that student motivation to read increased significantly in the more stimulating setting.

Another way to increase motivation to read and reading comprehension is through "authentic reading."

Authentic reading in science parallels the purposes that scientists have for reading—for example, reading to answer one's questions or reading to figure out the best way to proceed in an experiment. Thus authentic reading is tied to finding information or learning science processes. Duke and her colleagues (2006) followed the reading in science activities of a group of students from second through third grade. They found that students who experienced more authenticity in the purpose of reading and in the type of books used in science class grew more in reading comprehension. Thus teachers can support reading growth by providing stimulating activities and authentic reading opportunities in science class.

How can reading support science learning?

The instructional strategies and approaches used for reading in science can also impact student science learning. Guzzetti and her research team (1993) analyzed 23 reading research studies and 47 science education research studies and found that when reading and science strategies or approaches included some form of cognitive conflict, large effects were achieved. In other words, challenging students' prior conceptions resulted in increased learning. Researchers in both reading and science promote a sequence of instructional steps that taps into students' prior ideas and challenges students to shift these ideas through instruction.

Reading opportunities can be provided at different stages of the science learning cycle to help students build science knowledge. Integration of hands-on (firsthand) investigations with text-based (secondhand) investigations is supported by a number of research studies (Palincsar and Magnusson 2001). One interesting example comes from Romance and Vitale (2001), who studied classrooms grades 2–5 where literacy instruction was replaced by a daily two-hour block "dedicated solely to in-depth science concept instruction that encompassed reading comprehension and language arts skills (e.g., concept-focused teaching, hands-on activities, utilization of science-process skills, reading of science print materials, concept map construction, journal writing)" (p. 373). This integration of science and reading produced growth in science knowledge, reading comprehension, and attitudes and self-confidence toward both reading and science.

Is providing time for good science books enough?

Students do not necessarily learn to read by reading alone. Reading researchers have developed and tested a number of strategies that teachers can use to help students make sense of text. These strategies include activating background knowledge, predicting, goal setting, questioning, imagery, monitoring, and summarizing and can take place before, during, and after reading (Kragler, Walker, and Martin 2005; Yopp and Yopp 2006). In a study of four second-grade classrooms using science information texts, Reutzel, Smith, and Fawson (2005) compared the use of explicit teaching of these strategies singly versus teaching the strategies as a set using an engaging routine. The two variations produced no difference in reading comprehension; both groups improved their reading scores. However, using the set of comprehension strategies resulted in better science content acquisition than using the strategies individually. Teaching students strategies for reading for information can improve both reading comprehension and science learning.

How can we make the most of reading in science?

Science textbooks do not provide authentic reading experiences for students, nor do they give teachers much guidance on useful ways to help students read for information. That's what Kragler, Walker, and Martin (2005) found when they examined three different science textbook series at each grade level. This means that science teachers will need to go beyond the textbook to enhance science reading opportunities. Here are some research-based methods to make the most of reading in science:

- Select quality information and procedural books to coincide with your science units;

- Ask students to read in science for authentic purposes (e.g., to answer a question);

- Integrate firsthand science experiences with secondhand reading experiences;

- In both reading and science, create cognitive conflict that will lead to conceptual understanding; and

- Use comprehension strategies before, during, and after reading to help students make sense of text.

References

Duke, N. K., V. Purcell-Gates, L. A. Hall, and C. Tower. 2006. Authentic literacy activities for developing comprehension and writing: Explore what is meant by "authentic" literacy and discover how this approach can spark reading and writing across genres and subject areas. *The Reading Teacher* 60 (4): 344–356.

Gagnon, M. J., and S. K. Abell. 2007. Making time for science talk. *Science and Children* 44 (8): 66–67.

Guthrie, J. T., K. C. Perencevich, A. Wigfield, A. Taboada, N. M. Humenick, and P. Barbosa. 2006. Influences of stimulating tasks on reading motivation and comprehension. *The Journal of Educational Research* 99 (4): 232–245.

Guzzetti, B. J., T. E. Snyder, G. V. Glass, and W. S. Gamas. 1993. Promoting conceptual change in science: A comparative meta-analysis of instructional interventions from reading education and science education. *Reading Research Quarterly* 28 (2): 116–159.

Kragler, S., C. A. Walker, and L.A. Martin. 2005. Strategy instruction in primary content textbooks. *The Reading Teacher* 59 (3): 254–261.

Norris, S. P., and L. M. Phillips. 2003. How literacy is fundamental to science literacy. *Science Education* 87 (2): 224–240.

Palincsar, A., and S. Magnusson. 2001. The interplay of firsthand and text-based investigations to model and support the development of scientific knowledge and reasoning. In *Cognition and instruction: Twenty-five years of progress*, eds. S. Carver and D. Klahr, pp. 151–193. Mahwah, NJ: Erlbaum.

Reutzel, D. R., J. A. Smith, and P. C. Fawson. 2005. An evaluation of two approaches for teaching reading comprehension strategies in the primary years using science information texts. *Early Childhood Research Quarterly* 20 (3): 276–305.

Romance, N. R., and M. R. Vitale. 2001. Implementing an in-depth expanded science model in elementary schools: Multi-year findings, research issues, and policy implications. *International Journal of Science Education* 23 (4): 373–404.

Yopp, H. K., and R. H. Yopp. 2006. Primary students and informational texts. *Science and Children* 44 (3): 22–25.

12

The Synergy of Science and Reading

By Tracy L. Coskie

"Elementary teachers today are faced with a lot of pressure to focus their efforts on teaching reading. Often this means that other disciplines, such as science, are squeezed in or (worse) left out completely. Is it possible that teaching science can actually support reading? Can reading effectively support an inquiry approach to science? What is the evidence that integrating science and literacy leads to successful outcomes for students?"

How can science support learning to read?

Most of us approach reading tasks with a purpose—to plan a vacation or to get caught up on the news, for example. Our purposes and our engagement in the ideas and experiences related to our reading motivate us to make sense of what we read. Guthrie and Wigfield have been studying the effects of linking instruction in reading strategies with supports for engagement. Because the engage-

ment strategies include focusing on content goals and providing hands-on activities, they are particularly well suited to science. In one set of studies (Guthrie et al. 2004) the group embedded this "concept oriented reading instruction" in a science unit on ecology in life science. Students receiving this kind of instruction outperformed students receiving either traditional instruction or focused reading strategy instruction on tests of reading comprehension.

Other studies have shown that science and reading integration leads to improved comprehension (Brown and Campione 1998; Morrow et al. 1997). Perhaps this is not surprising. Consider that students who come to a reading task with some prior knowledge of the topic are more likely to understand and remember what they read (NRP 2000). Inquiry-based science experiences help students build prior knowledge and encounter concrete examples of vocabulary concepts. Of course, as students reencounter those concepts through talk and text, their understandings expand and deepen.

How can reading support science learning?

In the past, reading often took the place of students' own hands-on work with science ideas. Used appropriately, however, text can facilitate students' learning throughout the inquiry process. Well-written science trade books, for example, introduce new ideas and can be the motivating catalyst for engaging in exploration. Reading can also provide students with important opportunities for secondhand investigations (Palincsar and Magnusson 2001), helping students extend their new understandings as they enter the elaboration phase, as well as giving students access to explorations that are impossible for students to replicate in classrooms.

The National Science Foundation recently has funded development of the Seeds of Science/Roots of Reading curriculum. In their work, Cervetti et al. (2006) have found that texts can model the nature and processes of science, sharing with readers the questioning, inquiry strategies, uses of evidence, and making of conclu-

sions in which real scientific thinkers engage. Field trials of their curriculum have shown that not only does the integration support vocabulary development and reading comprehension but also students show significantly greater growth on measures of science learning than those students involved in a strict inquiry-only approach.

How are science and reading synergistic?

One of the key findings cited in *How People Learn* (Donovan, Bransford, and Pellegrino 1999) is that "the teaching of metacognitive skills should be integrated into the curriculum in a variety of subject areas" (p. 17). For example, we want to foster students' abilities to draw inferences and make connections as they engage in scientific inquiry. These are important thinking strategies that also support comprehension in reading. Because of the way these thinking strategies are applied in text reading versus science investigations, students who are taught explicitly to engage in these ways of thinking in both contexts become more aware of their strategies and more purposeful and flexible in their use. In a review of research on metacognitive strategies in reading and science, Baker (2004) tells us that, "To the extent that science and literacy draw on many of the same cognitive and metacognitive processes, cross-curricular connections may well have a synergistic effect in promoting development" (p. 254).

As these shared strategies suggest, integrating reading and science holds promise for improved student achievement. Programs designed to explore this integration have shown that students are motivated to engage in the work. Furthermore, they develop positive attitudes toward both reading and science (Anderson et al. 1997). Studies of programs specifically developed to link science and literacy have also begun providing further evidence that student achievement is greater in well-integrated programs than in traditional approaches that teach science and reading as separate subjects (Cervetti et al. 2006; Romance and Vitale 2001). Given the need elementary teachers have to make the most efficient and effective use of their curricular time, research in this area shows that sharing reading instruction time with that of science inquiry is time well spent.

References

Anderson, T. H., C. K.West, D. P. Beck, E. S. MacDonell, and D. S. Frisbie. 1997. Integrating reading and science education: On developing and evaluating WEE Science. *Journal of Curriculum Studies* 29 (6): 711–733.

Baker, L. 2004. Reading comprehension and science inquiry: Metacognitive connections. In *Crossing borders in literacy and science instruction,* ed. E. W. Saul, 239–257. Newark, DE and Arlington, VA: International Reading Association/National Science Teachers Association.

Brown, A. L., and J. C. Campione. 1998. Designing a community of young learners: Theoretical and practical lessons. In *How students learn: Reforming schools through learner-centered education*, eds. N. M. Lambert and B. L. McCombs, 153–186. Washington, DC: American Psychological Association.

Cervetti, G. N., P. D. Pearson, M. A. Bravo, and J. Barber. 2006. Reading and writing in the service of inquiry-based science. In *Linking science and literacy in the K–8 classroom,* eds. R. Douglas, K. Worth, and W. Binder, 199–222. Arlington, VA: NSTA Press.

Donovan, M. S., J. D. Bransford, and J. W. Pellegrino. 1999. *How people learn: Bridging research and practice.* Washington, DC: National Academies Press.

Guthrie, J. T., A. Wigfield, P. Barbosa, K. C. Perencevich, A. Taboada, M. Davis, N. Scaffidi, and S. Tonks. 2004. Increasing reading comprehension and engagement through concept-oriented reading instruction. *Journal of Educational Psychology* 96 (3): 402–423.

Morrow, L. M., M. Pressley, J. K. Smith, and M. Smith. 1997. The effect of a literature-based program integrated into literacy and science instruction with children from diverse backgrounds. *Reading Research Quarterly* 32: 54–76.

National Reading Panel (NRP). 2000. *Teaching children to read: An evidence-based assessment of the scientific research literature on reading and its implications for reading instruction*. Washington, DC:

National Institute of Child Health and Human Development.

Palincsar, A. S., and S. J. Magnusson. 2001. The interplay of firsthand and text-based investigations to model and support the development of scientific knowledge and reasoning. In *Cognition and instruction: Twenty-five years of progress,* eds. S. Carver and D. Klahr, 151–194. Mahwah, NJ: Lawrence Erlbaum.

Romance, N. R., and M. R. Vitale. 2001. Implementing an in-depth expanded science model in elementary schools: Multi-year findings, research issues, and policy implications. *International Journal of Science Education* 23 (4): 373–404.

13

Children's Literature and the Science Classroom

By Sandra K. Abell

"I often start my unit planning by going to the media center and checking out all the children's books I can find on a topic. But sometimes I worry that these are not the best books and that I am not using them in the best ways."

Why should I use children's literature in science class?

Elementary students can read about science in order to learn new content, to gain new science-process skills, and to increase their motivation to read. One way to achieve these goals, in addition to firsthand science experiences, is to engage students in reading beyond the science textbook. Children's literature, or trade books, address many scientific topics, both in narrative (story-based) and expository (informational) forms. Books take children to places that they could not go on their own and allow them to explore natural phenomena that might be too small or take too long to observe directly in the classroom. They provide a context for developing process skills (Monhardt and Monhardt 2006) and help create a sense of place (Wells and Zeece 2007). Children's books are often more fun to read than a dry textbook, they can accommodate a wide variety of reading skills and learning styles, and they are often more up-to-date and inclusive of women and minorities than textbooks (Rice 2002). However, teachers need to use caution when selecting books for a given science unit.

What are some problems with the science in children's literature?

A number of researchers have studied the science content in children's literature with disappointing results. Marriott (2002) examined 1,074 children's books with a nature theme, including 996 narrative books and 78 expository books. He found that the majority of books portrayed domesticated mammals only; when wild animals did appear, rarely were they seen in their natural habitats. Furthermore, animal characters were typically anthropomorphized by the authors. Trundle and Troland (2005) evaluated 79 children's books in which the Moon appeared prominently in text or illustrations. They found that many books misrepresented the Moon pictorially and reinforced misconceptions about Moon phases. Rice and Rainsford (Rice 2002) conducted a content analysis of 50 commonly used children's books with science themes, including 28 expository books and 22 narratives. They found many errors in drawings and misinformation in the texts. For example, slugs were identified as bugs, camouflage variations were exaggerated, and quicksand was presented as only found in jungles. Several authors have suggested criteria for the selection of children's literature for the science classroom. Sudol and King (1996) developed a checklist with five sections for evaluating expository trade books: accuracy, organization and layout, cohesion of ideas, specialized vocabulary, and reader interest. Pringle and Lamme (2005) provided a set of criteria for judging both narrative and expository books for science that included

accurate science content, terminology, and illustrations; proportionality and magnification made obvious; and well-written and entertaining. But what is the relationship between the quality of the content in children's literature and children's development of science concepts?

What science do children learn from children's literature?

Two researchers have studied how children learn science from children's literature. In the first study, Mayer (1995) read a narrative account of whales individually to 16 children from kindergarten through third grade. In the book, the main character addresses and corrects a little girl's misconceptions about whales. After reading the book to each child, Mayer asked the child to retell the story and answer a set of questions. What she found was surprising. Children remembered the erroneous ideas held by the girl instead of the correct information related by the main character. Rice (2002) and her colleagues took Mayer's study further. They read five books about whales to two classes of second graders and one class of fourth graders, preceded and followed by a series of true/false questions. They found that students had some prior knowledge about whales from their pretest answers. In analyzing posttest results, the researchers found that children did not change their answers to most questions. However, when they did change their answers, it was to mirror the information in the book that was read to them, whether correct or incorrect. In both of these studies, the researchers found that children do remember information presented in books, whether accurate or not. This implies that teachers have a critical role to play in helping students learn science with children's literature.

How can I use children's literature in science effectively?

The first step is to find the best books for your science unit. Several researchers provide examples of scientifically accurate books for teaching specific topics (see Barclay, Benelli, and Schoon 1999: Marriott 2002; Pringle and Lamme 2005; and Wells and Zeece 2007). Also, every March *Science and Children* publishes the list of "Outstanding Trade Books for Children" selected by NSTA and the Children's Book Council. Once you have some books to use in your unit, you might consider how best to use the books. One idea is to use children's literature to motivate children for a science study. Another idea is to use the books during the concept introduction phase

of the learning cycle (Brown and Abell 2007), after students have engaged in firsthand experiences with a phenomenon. Some researchers have suggested that books with scientific errors can actually provide fruitful avenues of study. For example, Trundle and Troland (2005) suggest that, when studying the Moon, teachers can have children make regular observations of the Moon phases and then follow up by comparing their observations with illustrations in various books. According to Rice (2002), using children's literature in this way can help children become critical readers, questioning the accuracy of what they read.

References

Barclay, D., C. Benelli, and S. Schoon. 1999. Marking the connection! Science and literacy. *Childhood Education* 75 (3): 146–152.

Brown, P. L., and S. K. Abell. 2007. Examining the learning cycle. *Science and Children* 44 (5): 58–59.

Marriott, S. 2002. Red in tooth and claw? Images of nature in modern picture books. *Children's Literature in Education* 33 (3): 175–183.

Mayer, D. A. 1995. How can we best use children's literature in teaching science concepts? *Science and Children* 32 (6): 16–19, 43.

Monhardt, L., and R. Monhardt. 2006.

Creating a context for the learning of science process skills through picture books. *Early Childhood Education Journal* 34 (1): 67–71.

Pringle, R. M., and L. L. Lamme. 2005. Using picture storybooks to support young children's science learning, *Reading Horizons* 46 (1): 1–15.

Rice, D. C. 2002. Using trade books in teaching elementary science: Facts and fallacies. *The Reading Teacher* 55 (6): 552–565.

Sudol, P., and C. M. King. 1996. A checklist for choosing nonfiction trade books. *The Reading Teacher* 49 (5): 422–424.

Trundle, K. C., and T. H. Troland. 2005. The Moon in children's literature. *Science and Children* 43 (2): 40–43.

Wells, R., and P. D. Zeece. 2007. My place in my world: Literature for place-based environmental education. *Early Childhood Education Journal* 35 (3): 285–291.

14

On Writing in Science

By Sandra K. Abell

"My fourth graders write all the time in science. They record Purpose, Equipment, Procedures, and Results in their science notebooks for every activity. But lately they seem to resist writing. I'm thinking of dropping the writing—it just takes too much time. After all, they just need to learn science in science class."

Why use writing in science?

Many teachers use writing in science as a recording tool (science notebooks) or to find out what students have learned (constructed-response tests). Yet writing experts Judith Langer and Arthur Applebee (1987) tell us that writing to evaluate knowledge and skills is only one of several purposes for writing. According to their framework, writing in science classrooms can also: (1) draw on prior knowledge to prepare for new activities; (2) foster new learning; (3) consolidate and review ideas; and (4) reformulate and extend knowledge.

Can writing help students understand science better?

One of the most important reasons for using writing in science is to foster conceptual understanding. Mason and Boscolo (2000) studied Italian fourth-grade student writing in science. Students who engaged in writing to reflect, reason, and compare understood photosynthesis better than students who did not write to learn. Fellows (1994) found that urban middle school students who had more opportunities for writing explanations produced better logical arguments and changed their concepts about matter and molecules. Other studies have shown that students who write to explain their ideas learn science better than students who write only to record or summarize (Hand, Prain, and Yore 2001).

What supports do students need for science writing?

Many students find it easier to express their ideas through talking than writing. In a study by Warwick, Linfield, and Stephenson (1999), 11-year-olds were able to express clear understanding of fair testing and other experimental design ideas in interview settings, but those ideas were less apparent in students' written work. However, teachers can help all students become better writers and better science learners by teaching them how to write scientifically. Warwick, Stephenson, and Webster (2003) found that the writing of fourth-grade students in England reflected high levels of understanding of ideas like variables and fair testing after teachers provided a writing frame with prompts such as: "We are trying to find out … We made the test fair by … ." (p. 176). Working with second-grade students in Wales, Patterson (2001) found that when teachers provided explicit instruction in writing, students were able to express greater scientific understanding. For example, when teachers showed students how to use connectives (words like *for, to, when, because*) in their science writing, students moved from descriptions like "It has dots" to explanations like "It has got dots for bugs to eat" (p. 9).

Thus, teaching writing techniques led students to express more thorough understanding.

How can teachers provide feedback on student science writing?

Owens (2001) found that elementary teachers are often frustrated about how to respond to science writing—Do we respond to the ideas or the writing? If students use the right words, does that mean they understand? How will my comments affect student learning?

How teachers respond to student writing will depend on the purpose of the writing. If writing is aimed at building science understanding, then teacher responses need to push for clarity in explanation and point out discrepancies in thinking. Teachers should not accept the right word as a substitute for conceptual understanding. For example, a student who writes, "Things float because of their density" might understand, or may just be making "noises that sound scientific" (Osborne and Freyberg 1985) without understanding that an object's mass and volume are both important considerations in sinking and floating. Teacher responses to science writing will help students become better writers and thinkers (Spandel and Stiggins 1990). In the density example, responses such as "What do you mean by density? Can you give an example? What about things that sink?" will help students move beyond vocabulary to conceptual understanding.

Should all students be expected to write in science?

All students can be involved in writing in science. For kindergarteners, science writing might include pictures and invented spelling. Even in second grade, students can improve their science thinking and writing when teachers provide writing supports such as concept maps (Patterson 2001).

What can teachers do to help students write to learn science?

Instead of merely writing about science, students need to engage in writing to learn science (Owens 2001). Writing to learn helps students build their knowledge through conjecture, explanation, comparison, and reformulation. Teachers can do the following to help students learn science better through writing:

- Ask students to write in science every day.

- Expect all students to be successful writers in science.

- Provide writing tasks that go beyond recording and summarizing.

- Include writing prompts that help students structure their writing.

- Respond to writing with direct feedback about the science ideas.

In these ways, writing and thinking become essential components of the elementary science classroom.

References

Fellows, N. J. 1994. A window into thinking: Using student writing to understand conceptual change in science learning. *Journal of Research in Science Teaching* 31 (9): 985–1001.

Hand, B., V. Prain, and L. Yore. 2001. Sequential writing tasks' influence on science learning. In *Writing as a learning tool: Integrating theory and practice*, eds. P. Tynjala, L. Mason, and K. Lonka. Dordrecht, The Netherlands: Kluwer.

Langer, J. A., and A. N. Applebee. 1987. *How writing shapes thinking: A study of teaching and learning*. Urbana, IL: National Council of Teachers of English.

Mason, L., and P. Boscolo. 2000. Writing and conceptual change: What changes? *Instructional Science* 28 (3): 199–226.

Osborne, R., and P. Freyberg. 1985. *Learning in science: The implications of children's science*. Portsmouth, NH: Heinemann.

Owens, C. V. 2001. Teachers' responses to science writing. *Teaching and Learning: The Journal of Natural Inquiry.* Summer: 22–35.

Patterson, E. W. 2001. Structuring the composition process in scientific writing. *International Journal of Science Education* 23 (1): 1–16.

Spandel, V., and R. J. Stiggins. 1990. *Creating writers: Linking assessment and writing instruction.* White Plains, NY: Longman.

Warwick, P., R. S. Linfield, and P. Stephenson.1999. A comparison of primary school pupils' ability to express procedural understanding in science through speech and writing. *International Journal of Science Education* 21 (8): 823–838.

Warwick, P., P. Stephenson, and J. Webster. 2003. Developing pupils' written expression of procedural understanding through the use of writing frames in science: Findings from a case study approach. *International Journal of Science Education* 25 (2): 173–192.

Student
Thinking and
Misconceptions

15

Assessing and Addressing Student Science Ideas

By S. Rená Smith and Sandra K. Abell

"A colleague and I were talking about our recent science units. He mentioned that several of his students still had some 'wacky' ideas about certain concepts. I noticed from my pre- and posttests that a few of my students still had misconceptions too. What can we do to assess and address students' science ideas?"

Where do students' "wacky" science ideas come from?

Our students are not blank slates. They come to school with a wide range of experiences that have shaped their science understandings—reading books, watching TV, playing video games. Sometimes these sources get the science wrong (for example, the popular Pokemon game uses the term *evolution* instead of *metamorphosis* when referring to creatures going through life stages). In a study of 79 children's books, Trundle and Troland (2005) found that many books reinforced misconceptions about Moon phases and contained incorrect pictorial representations. Everyday language also contributes to scientific misunderstandings. Phrases such as "shut the door or you'll let the heat out" can cause students to think that heat is a substance, not a form of energy. Interactions with phenomena can lead to inaccurate scientific understandings. For example, although any two objects will fall at the same speed in a vacuum, in everyday life a feather falls more slowly than a coin because of air resistance. Finally, students can construct inaccurate meanings from science instruction itself. Students can ignore teacher talk, use "noises that sound scientific" to represent incomplete understanding, or be confused by mismatches between their language and the teacher's (Osborne and Freyberg 1985). From many years of research about student science ideas, we know that student science misconceptions are prevalent, strongly held, and highly resistant to change.

How do I find out what misconceptions my students hold?

Researchers have used a number of strategies to assess student science ideas. The most common strategy is the individual interview (Osborne and Freyburg 1985). Interviewers ask students to explain phenomena and probe for more information. Or they provide words and pictures for students to sort based on their understanding of concepts like animal, living, matter, and electricity. However, the individual interview strategy may not be practical for the classroom. Other useful tools for assessing student science ideas include the two-tiered test (in which a multiple-choice item is followed by the opportunity to explain one's reasoning), open-ended questions that lead to children writing and drawing about their ideas, and concept maps. Page Keeley and her colleagues (2005, 2007) designed a set of formative assessment probes to uncover student ideas. However, the simplest way to assess student ideas might be to listen to the students during class discussions and pay attention to what they write and draw in their science notebooks.

What misconceptions can I expect?

Teachers do not have to interview or test every student to find out their ideas—many science misconceptions are quite common and can be predicted. The internet is a valuable resource for delineating possible student misconceptions before the start of a unit. For example, some university science teacher educators have websites that list student science ideas (Hanuscin 2001). Some researchers have compiled the findings from numerous studies of children's ideas in various science topic areas (see Driver et al. 1994). Other books describe in-depth studies of student learning in one area, like Shapiro's (1994) study of fifth graders learning about light. Some science curriculum materials also list common student misconceptions. For example, in a unit about force and motion, it is common for many students to think that a force is needed to keep an object that is moving in motion; students also have trouble understanding how a wall or a table can exert a force on their hands. When teachers are aware of these areas of potential difficulties, they can begin to plan instruction that will address student misconceptions.

What strategies can I use to address students' misconceptions?

There is widespread agreement among science education researchers that the first step in students changing their conceptual understanding is becoming dissatisfied with their current ideas. Activities that challenge students' ideas, such as discrepant events, create disequilibrium that students want to resolve. Furthermore, students need to be presented with new concepts that are reasonable and meaningful to them (Shapiro 1994). Many researchers have found that a learning cycle approach (Brown and Abell 2007), with opportunities for exploration and science talk, can lead to conceptual change. For example, Gang (1995) found that using a learning cycle with middle school students to help them understand Archimedes' principle was more effective than traditional presentation and demonstration. Hardy and colleagues (2006) investigated third-grade student learning about floating and sinking. They found that students who received high instructional support in the form of discussion, reflection, and connecting concepts developed more coherent understandings of floating and sinking than students with less instructional support. Maria (1997) followed one boy from kindergarten through third grade, tracking his understanding of the causes of day and night and the seasons. Developmentally appropriate instructional scaffolds (e.g., exploring models, engaging in hands-on activities, and discussing what he read) helped him restructure his ideas. Good science instruction can lead to conceptual change—that's what Trundle and her colleagues found (2007) when studying fourth graders learning about phases of the Moon. What we learn from all of these researchers is that when students actively participate in science by doing and thinking and communicating, conceptual change is possible.

References

Brown, P. L., and S. K. Abell. 2007. Examining the learning cycle. *Science and Children* 44 (5): 58–59.

Driver, R., A. Squires, P. Rushworth, and V. Wood-Robinson. 1994. *Making sense of secondary science*. London: Routledge.

Gang, S. 1995. Removing Preconceptions with a "Learning Cycle." *The Physics Teacher* 33: 346–354.

Hanuscin, D. 2001. *Misconceptions in science E328: Elementary methods.* Available online at *www.indiana. edu/~w505a/studwork/deborah/ index.html.*

Hardy, I., E. Stern, A. Jonen, and K. Moller. 2006. Effects of instructional support within constructivist learning environments for elementary school students' understanding of "floating and sinking." *Journal of Educational Psychology* 98 (2): 307–326.

Keeley, P., F. Eberle, and L. Farrin. 2005. *Uncovering student ideas in science, volume 1: 25 formative assessment probes.* Arlington, VA: NSTA Press.

Keeley, P., F. Eberle, and J. Tugel. 2007. *Uncovering student ideas in science, volume 2: 25 more formative assessment probes.* Arlington, VA: NSTA Press.

Maria, K. 1997. A case study of conceptual change in a young child.

The Elementary School Journal 98 (1): 67–88.

Osborne, R., and P. Freyberg. 1985. *Learning in science: The implications of children's science.* Portsmouth, NH: Heinemann.

Shapiro, B. 1994. *What children bring to light: A constructivist perspective on children's learning in science.* New York: Teachers College Press.

Trundle, K. C., R. K. Atwood, and J. E. Christopher. 2007. Fourth-grade elementary students' conceptions of standards-based lunar concepts. *International Journal of Science Education* 29 (5): 595–616.

Trundle, K. C., and T. H. Troland. 2005. The Moon in children's literature. *Science and Children* 43 (2): 40–43.

16

Assessing for Science Learning

By Michele H. Lee and Sandra K. Abell

"My principal has suggested that I include more assessment in my teaching. However, I simply don't see how more tests and quizzes are going to help my students learn science."

What is formative assessment, and how does it differ from summative assessment?

Often the word *assessment* conjures up the notion of tests or quizzes that occur at the end of a lesson or a unit. These summative assessments take place when an instructional sequence is completed, providing a summary of what students learned. The summative information reports a student's status for purposes of grading, evaluation, or certification. Although results may be provided to parents, school districts, and other external agencies, these results typically have minimal bearing on classroom instruction and student learning. In contrast, formative assessment is used to gain

information that improves instruction and advances student learning. Just as a doctor diagnoses symptoms before determining how to alleviate them, a teacher must diagnose student ideas before determining how to help students learn scientific ideas (Osborne and Freyberg 1985). Following initial diagnosis, a doctor must monitor treatment effects and gauge the patient's status. In the classroom, a teacher uses formative assessment to gather data about the effectiveness of past instruction (McNair 2004) and inform future instruction. Formative assessment entails both "gathering information about children's ongoing development of ideas and skills and using this in modifying activities and the teacher's interventions to meet the children's needs" (Harlen 2001, p. 64). This process of gathering and using information about student understanding is thus ongoing and cyclical.

How does formative assessment benefit students?

According to cognitive scientists, people learn science better if they are metacognitive about their learning (NRC 2005)—when they recognize what they know and do not know and decide what they need to learn. Teachers who regularly use formative assessment to provide feedback to their students can improve student metacognition, because feedback engages students in thinking about their learning and progress. Feedback enables students to recognize the strengths and weaknesses in their work and know what they can do to meet the expected level of performance or understanding (Sadler 1989). Teacher feedback that centers on individual improvement can foster an expectation of success for all (Black and Wiliam 1998). Bergan et al. (1991) found that kindergartners achieved significantly higher science test scores in classrooms where teachers used assessments to inform and differentiate instruction to match individual student needs than did students in classrooms where a formative assessment program was not in place.

What strategies for formative assessment in science are most effective?

When formative assessment is integrated seamlessly throughout the learning experience (Volkmann and Abell 2003), instruction and assessment are indivisible (Black and Wiliam 1998; NRC 2000). Effective instruction integrates formative assessment when teachers require students to write, draw, and speak in response to questions and problem situations. Predicting activities, end-of-class reflective writing, concept maps, scientists, meetings, and science notebook tasks provide contexts for students to try out their developing understanding and receive feedback from the teacher. The kinds of questions that teachers ask in these formative assessment settings make a difference. Bell, Osborne, and Tasker (1985) interviewed elementary students about their science ideas (about plants, animals, and electricity) using open-ended questions (e.g., What do you think … ? Can you explain to me the way you think … ?). These questions required students to reason and express their ideas, and their answers enabled the researchers to discern student misunderstandings. The researchers advised teachers to ask appropriate questions and listen carefully to student answers, asking follow-up questions that require students to explain more, such as Why do you think that?

Teacher responses to student questions also influence student learning (Osborne and Simon 1996). Budd Rowe (2003) found that when teachers give more time for students to respond (five seconds or longer) after asking a question, more students respond, give longer responses, are less likely to say "I don't know," and are more likely to engage in speculative thinking and provide arguments based on evidence. Information gained in such exchanges allows teachers to adjust lessons to provide students with new opportunities to reason.

How can teachers begin to implement effective formative assessment strategies?

Formative assessment helps teachers understand students' prior knowledge, knowledge/skill development, misunderstandings, and learning difficulties, and adapt teaching to meet student needs while at the same time including students in understanding learning expectations (NRC 2001). Frequent formative assessment and feedback to students about their learning can improve student achievement (Black and Wiliam 1998) and inform teachers about the effects of their instruction. We offer a few suggestions for improving formative assessment in elementary science classrooms:

- Figure out the most important ideas that you want students to learn, help students recognize your learning purposes, and plan ways to revisit their ideas throughout a unit of instruction.

- Design a variety of formative assessments that involve different types of student performances— writing, drawing, inventing, and speaking.

- Implement some type of formative assessment in each lesson.

- Carefully listen to and observe the ways students develop and display their understandings.

- Think about what you learn from the results of the formative assessment as you plan subsequent lessons.

References
Bell, B., R. Osborne, and R. Tasker. 1985. Finding out what children think. In *Learning in science: The implications of children's science*, eds. R. Osborne and P. Freyberg (pp. 151–165). Portsmouth, NH: Heinemann.

Bergan, J. R., I. E. Sladeczek, R. D. Schwarz, and A. N. Smith. 1991. Effects of a measurement and planning system on kindergartners' cognitive development and educational programming, *American Educational Research Journal* 28 (3): 683–714.

Black, P., and D. Wiliam. 1998. Inside the black box: Raising standards through classroom assessment. *Phi Delta Kappan* 80 (2): 139–144.

Budd Rowe, M. 2003. Wait-time and rewards as instructional variables, their influence on language, logic, and fate control: Part one-wait-time [Reprint 1974]. *Journal of Research in Science Teaching* 40 (1): S19–32.

Harlen, W. 2001. Research in primary science education. *Journal of Biological Education* 35 (2): 61–65.

McNair, S. 2004. "A" is for assessment. *Science and Children* 42 (1): 24–27.

National Research Council (NRC). 2000. *Inquiry and the national science education standards.* Washington, DC: National Academies Press.

National Research Council (NRC). 2001. *Classroom assessment and the national science education standards.* Washington, DC: National Academy Press.

National Research Council (NRC). 2005. *How students learn: Science in the classroom.* Washington, DC: National Academies Press.

Osborne, J., and S. Simon. 1996. Primary science: Past and future directions. *Studies in Science Education* 27: 99–147.

Osborne, R. J., and P. Freyberg. 1985. *Learning in science: The implications of children's science.* Portsmouth, NH: Heinemann.

Sadler, R. 1989. Formative assessment and the design of instructional systems. *Instructional Science* 18 (2): 119–144.

Volkmann, M. J., and S. K. Abell. 2003. Seamless assessment. *Science and Children* 40 (8): 41–45.

17

Thinking About Thinking in Science Class

By Sandra K. Abell

"The other day during our electricity unit, I heard one of my students say, 'Your idea makes more sense than mine.' How can I encourage more of this thinking about thinking in science class?"

Why is thinking about thinking important in science class?

Our science students come to science class with ideas about how the world works—ideas that are often different from accepted scientific ideas. Teachers work hard to help students rethink their ideas through a process of conceptual change, but the students themselves have an important role to play. Students regulate their own learning. Self-regulated learners are able to set learning goals, find strategies that help them achieve those goals, and monitor their progress (Schraw, Crippen, and Hartley 2006). An important part of self-regulation is thinking about thinking, or metacognition. According to cognitive

scientists (Donovan and Bransford 2005), metacognition involves self-monitoring and reflection on learning. Researchers have shown that metacognition can support student learning with understanding in many subjects. How does metacognition support science learning?

Can metacognition support conceptual change in science?

The work of Sister Gertrude Hennessey (2003) in teaching and researching elementary science has shown that children's metacognitive abilities are essential to conceptual change in science. In a series of studies with first through sixth graders, Hennessey developed strategies for helping students be metacognitive, implemented them in her teaching, and listened closely to students as they learned science. During science class, she asked students questions like, *Can you state your own ideas? Can you talk about why you are attracted to your idea?* (Beeth 1998). Hennessey found that children of all ages could become aware of and regulate their own thinking processes. Furthermore, through self-interrogation and introspection, students came to understand the scientific ideas more deeply. For example, in a fifth-grade unit on the particulate nature of matter, students used their metacognitive skills to help reason about states of matter using water as a case example (Beeth 1998). One of the students recognized that the various explanations the class had developed for differences in solid and liquid water were inconsistent, which helped the class come to a deeper understanding of states of matter. Hennessey's work as a science teacher and a researcher demonstrates that teachers can help students become more metacognitive and that thinking about thinking improves conceptual understanding in science.

What are other benefits of thinking about thinking in science class?

Not only do we want our science students to develop more accurate scientific ideas, we want their new understandings to transfer to other situations and to be durable over time. Researchers have studied the impact of metacognitive instruction on the transfer and durability of conceptual understanding in science. Georghiades (2000) carried out a study of fifth graders learning about electricity in Cyprus. During the five-week unit, one group of students received instruction that included metacognitive activities while the other group the control group) did not. (The metacognitive instruction included questions for discussion and writing such as, "Before having this lesson, what was your belief regarding X? Have you changed your views? ... Write down three things you learned during today's lesson" (p. 131). Teachers also asked students in the metacognitive group to use drawing and concept mapping to express their ideas. Although all students showed immediate benefit from the electricity unit, eight months later the metacognitive group outperformed the control group overall and on tasks that required transfer to new situations. These results demonstrate that the inclusion of metacognitive activities improved both the transfer and durability of students' understanding of electricity. In a similar study of middle school student learning in an ecology unit, Blank (2000) found that the metacognitive group (who had time to formally discuss their science ideas in class), performed better in a delayed posttest, demonstrating greater durability of student understanding.

What are some strategies that I can incorporate into my science teaching to promote metacognition?

The National Research Council (Duschl, Schweingruber, and Shouse 2007) recommends that K–8 teachers use metacognitively guided learning in their science teaching. They suggest that teachers help students become aware of their initial science ideas, make predictions and provide reasons for their predictions, and discuss and compare their ideas with others. Keogh and Naylor (1999) offer a strategy to help students compare scientific ideas, the concept cartoon. A concept cartoon presents several viewpoints on a concept in a captivating way. Students think about how their ideas compare to those of the individuals in the cartoon. In their research, Keogh and Naylor found that elementary teachers thought the cartoons were useful in making students' ideas accessible to them during instruction. Metacognitive strategies can be integrated throughout instruction. Blank (2000) recommends a metacognitive learning cycle that includes explicit conceptual status checks to accompany each learning cycle phase (see Brown and Abell 2007). Schraw and his colleagues (2006) describe a set of instructional strategies to improve self-regulation in the science classroom, including inquiry, collaboration, and mental models. Within these strategies, teachers can promote metacognition by helping students plan and monitor investigations, evaluate explanations and models, and self-reflect on their learning. By using metacognitive teaching strategies, science teachers can help students regulate their learning, thereby achieving deeper and more durable scientific understanding.

References

Beeth, M. E. 1998. Teaching science in fifth grade: Instructional goals that support conceptual change. *Journal of Research in Science Teaching* 35 (10): 1091–1101.

Blank, L. M. 2000. A metacognitive learning cycle: A better warranty for student understanding. *Science Education* 84 (4): 486–506.

Brown, P. L., and S. K. Abell. 2007. Examining the learning cycle. *Science and Children* 44 (5): 58–59.

Dovovan, M. S., and J. D. Bransford. 2005. *How students learn: History, mathematics, and science in the classroom.* Washington, DC: National Academies Press.

Duschl, R. A., H. A. Schweingruber, and A. W. Shouse. 2007. *Taking science to school: Learning and teaching science in grades K–8*. Washington, DC: National Academies Press.

Georghiades, P. 2000. Beyond conceptual change learning in science education: Focusing on transfer, durability, and metacognition. *Educational Research* 42 (2): 119–139.

Hennessey, M. G. 2003. Metacognitive aspects of students' reflective discourse: Implications for intentional conceptual change teaching and learning. In *Intentional conceptual change,* eds. G. M. Sinatra and P. R. Pintrich, 103–132. Mahwah, NJ: Lawrence Erlbaum.

Keogh, B., and S. Naylor. 1999. Concept cartoons, teaching and learning in science: An evaluation. *International Journal of Science Education* 21 (4): 431–446.

Schraw, G., K. J. Crippen, and K. Hartley. 2006. Promoting self-regulation in science education: Metacognition as part of a broader perspective on learning. *Research in Science Education* 36 (1–2): 111–139.

18

The Myth of Catering to Learning Styles

By Joanne K. Olson

"The idea that people may have different abilities to learn, depending on the modality of instruction, has been around for over 100 years (Willingham 2005). When applied to educational practice, the essence of this viewpoint is that because everyone learns differently, we should teach students in multiple ways so that at least one of these modalities will match that of our learners, increasing the likelihood of learning. Better yet, we should preassess our students to determine their learning style and tailor lesson plans toward their preferred style. What evidence exists for these claims? Do 'kinesthetic learners' really need kinesthetic activities in order to learn?"

Does teaching to individual learning styles increase learning?

The idea that children learn best when instruction is tailored to their learning style is intuitively appealing and may seem to be supported by classroom experience. Some students appear to thrive when asked to express ideas through a role-play activity or through music. Others don't seem to understand an explanation until the teacher draws a picture or uses manipulatives to illustrate a concept.

However, research has shown that when students received instruction specifically tailored to their preferred learning style, they performed poorly on tests of the material (Salomon 1984). In fact, a comparison group who received instruction in formats different than their preferred style scored significantly better on the same tests!

Salomon found that the level of effort learners invested in the task was the critical factor that affected students' performance. When students received instruction in their preferred format, they exhibited overconfidence in their ability to learn the information, and thus, invested less effort in learning the content. This lower level of effort resulted in lower levels of learning. In contrast, when learners were confronted with instruction in a format different than that which they preferred, they perceived the task to be more difficult, exhibited greater effort to learn, and learned more as a result.

Other studies have also found no improvements when students are taught in their preferred style (Mayer and Massa 2003; Kavale and Forness 1987; Kampwirth and Bates 1980). In summary, "Researchers in this area have found no valid evidence that tailoring instruction to different learning styles results in any learning benefits" (Feldon 2005, p. 39).

How do teachers account for students' learning successes and difficulties?

When we understand similarities in how people learn, the better we understand why students may or may not learn science concepts. Consider these ideas:

Concrete representations should precede abstractions. In the 1700s, Rousseau noted that our ability to understand abstractions gradually develops over time, a finding supported empirically by Piaget in the mid-20th century. A verbal explanation may be difficult

for a child to understand, but when a more concrete representation (such as a picture or a real object) is used along with the explanation, the child has a greater likelihood of understanding.

For example, effective mathematics instruction often begins with concrete representations of the concept by using manipulatives. After students understand the concept using manipulatives, a symbolic representation using numerals is introduced. Similarly, in language arts, effective teachers begin a text with prereading strategies that help students use pictures and other visual cues prior to reading text.

In science, the same principle of beginning with concrete representations applies. The learning cycle and other inquiry-based instructional models emphasize that students need real experiences to precede more abstract development of concepts. Rather than beginning with text and doing the activity last, inquiry-based science instruction begins with experience, then develops concepts (using drawings, graphs, class discussion, and teacher-led instruction), and finally applies those concepts back to real experience. If text is used, it is after students have had rich experiences and have worked through their ideas.

Often, particular representations are required for students to understand a concept, not because it matches a student's learning "style" but because those representations are best suited to the content itself (Willingham 2005). In science, real experience with the natural phenomenon is critical in order to understand graphic representations or text. Learning about sound, for example, cannot be optimally accomplished without using sound. Willingham encourages teachers to select representations based on the nature of the concept. In this way, all children benefit.

As you prepare and teach a unit, ask yourself:

- What representations are best suited to this concept?

- How am I scaffolding my instruction from concrete toward more abstract representations?

- How abstract is this concept? How well can my students understand that level of abstraction?

New information is always filtered through prior knowledge. Teachers are often frustrated when carefully planned lessons result in partially understood (or completely misinterpreted) concepts by students. This is often due to the substantial role that prior knowledge and experience has on how students learn new information. Concepts that fit (or are perceived by the learner to fit) with prior information and experience are more readily grasped. Concepts too far from students' existing ideas are often memorized or ignored altogether.

Helping students deeply understand science concepts requires that we do more than become aware of students' prior knowledge. Students need to test their ideas, be introduced to scientific ideas, monitor how their thinking has changed, and see the utility of scientific ideas. The following questions can help as you prepare and teach science concepts:

- How does this content compare with students' prior experience?

- What words may be used in this unit that students have encountered before? How do they use these words?

- What misconceptions do students have about this concept?

- What prior knowledge is necessary in order to understand this concept?

In summary, teaching toward students' preferred learning styles has no solid basis in research and may lead to decreased effort and performance in the classroom. Using appropriate representations that carefully consider how to best convey the content is important. In addition, we need to scaffold between concrete and more abstract representations, being sensitive to the abilities of our students to handle abstractions. Finally, when students struggle to understand, we need to look at both the nature of the content as well as the prior experiences of our students. When we carefully select how we represent concepts and take into account students' thinking, we optimize learning opportunities for all of our students.

References

Feldon, D. F. 2005. Dispelling a few myths about learning. *UrbanEd* 1 (4): 37–39.

Kampwirth, T. J., and M. Bates. 1980. Modality preference and teaching method. A review of the research. *Academic Therapy* 15 (5): 597–605.

Kavale, K. A., and S. R. Forness. 1987. Substance over style: Assessing the efficacy of modality testing and teaching. *Exceptional Children* 54 (3): 228–239.

Mayer, R. E., and L. J. Massa. 2003. Three facets of visual and verbal learners: Cognitive ability, cognitive style, and learning preference. *Journal of Educational Psychology* 95 (4): 833–846.

Rousseau, J. 1979. *Emile or on education*. New York: Basic Books.

Salomon, G. 1984. Television is "easy" and print is "tough": The differential investment of mental effort in learning as a function of perceptions and attributions. *Journal of Educational Psychology* 76 (4): 647–658.

Willingham, D. T. 2005. Do visual, auditory, and kinesthetic learners need visual, auditory, and kinesthetic instruction? *American Educator* 29 (2): 31–35, 44.

19

A (Mis)Understanding of Astronomical Proportions?

By Michele H. Lee and Deborah L. Hanuscin

"When teaching astronomy, I've noticed my students have lots of incorrect ideas about the solar system. Despite the multiple hands-on activities and explanations of the scientific ideas included in our unit, students still hang onto their misconceptions. I don't have a strong background in astronomy myself, and wonder—What can I do to better assist students in learning astronomy concepts?"

What are some astronomy misconceptions common to elementary-age students?

Researchers over the past five decades have identified a number of commonly held misconceptions elementary students have about astronomy. For example, Klein (1982) studied second graders' ideas about night and day and found some believed the Sun "hides" at night. The majority of students failed to recognize the rotation of the Earth as the cause of night and day. Jones, Lynch, and Reesink (1987)

investigated students' conceptions of the shape, size, and motion of the Earth and Moon and found they held a variety of ideas, including some in which the Earth was the center of the solar system. Alternative notions of the phases of the moon have also been documented and include the ideas that clouds or other objects cast a shadow on the Moon (Baxter 1989).

Why might students hold incorrect ideas about astronomical events?

Often children's ideas derive from limited experience with objects in the sky. As *Benchmarks for Science Literacy* (AAAS 1993) emphasizes, students cannot determine how the solar system is put together just by looking at it. Telescopes provide some information to the earthbound viewer, and two-dimensional diagrams show what the system would look like if people could see it from far away, requiring students to put themselves outside of the system as they look in. However, students need three-dimensional models to make sense of the relationships among objects in the sky. Parker and Heywood (1998) found that students ages 7–11 often have difficulty interpreting two-dimensional diagrams that represent three-dimensional space. Other researchers (Nussbaum 1979; Parker and Heywood 1998) found that young children may become confused by ambiguous terminology, interpreting references to a "round Earth" to mean disk-shaped, versus spherical. Thus students may maintain ideas based on their limited astronomical experiences and knowledge when confronted with new explanations in the classroom (Hannust and Kikas 2007).

How can teachers address students' misconceptions?

In order to address students' astronomy misconceptions, it is critical that teachers use their students' ideas as a starting point for instruction. Akerson, Flick, and Lederman (2000) examined the practices of two experienced second-grade teachers and a student teacher during an astronomy unit, and identified several aspects of instruction that allowed students to express and reformulate their ideas through-out a lesson. For example, teachers elicited students' ideas using a cyclical pattern of open-ended questions to invite students to share ideas, probing questions to determine students' depth of understanding, and then responses that encouraged students to build on their ideas. To address specific misconceptions students had expressed about astronomy, the teachers (1) designed lessons with student ideas in mind, (2) demonstrated a concept using concrete objects such as balls to represent the position and motion of planets, (3) used nonfiction children's books to address specific ideas, (4) explained concepts using manipulatives or visual aids such as posters with movable planets, (5) scaffolded learning by using something familiar to students to link new ideas to old ones, such as relating "pierced ears" to cloud-piercing radar, and (6) discussed hands-on activities. In comparison, a student teacher who was teaching science for the first time and did not have a strong background in astronomy used strategies that unintentionally discouraged students' expression of ideas. Although she asked questions to invite students to share ideas, she did not follow up with probing questions. Good questioning strategies alone, however, may not be sufficient to gauge students' understanding. Schoultz, Saljo, and Wyndhamn (2001) interviewed elementary students about astronomical phenomena and found that relying on words alone, versus allowing students to manipulate concrete objects, produced markedly different student responses. Thus, providing students opportunities to *show*, not just explain, their ideas may enhance teachers' ability to elicit and build on students' ideas.

How can teachers better prepare themselves to address students' astronomy misconceptions?

An accurate and detailed understanding of astronomy concepts and how to represent them are keys to effective teaching. The NSTA Learning Center is one place to find reliable and accurate resources for teachers to strengthen their own content knowledge. In addition, during instruction it is also important for teachers to attend to students' misconceptions and possible sources of confusion. Dove (2000) recommends that teachers should

- use terminology correctly and encourage students to do the same, especially for commonly confused terms such as *orbit*, *spin*, and *turn*;

- assist students in becoming aware of misleading terminology (e.g., *new Moon* means "no Moon observable from Earth");

- help students recognize that diagrams and models are simplifications of reality and may misrepresent particular aspects, such as the size of the Moon in relation to the Earth when phases of the Moon are depicted;

- guide students in linking personal experiences with scientific ideas; for example, observing the face of the Moon during the month to check if it always presents the same perspective to the Earth;

- encourage students to use classroom models to demonstrate and explain their observations (e.g., using their hands to demonstrate astronomical movements as they verbally explain); and

- assess students in ways that require them to apply their knowledge rather than recite it.

Misconceptions are ideas formulated by children as they try to make sense of the world. By focusing on students' ideas, using the strategies suggested above, teachers can help students move toward more accurate understandings of the solar system.

References

Akerson, V. L., L. B. Flick, and N. G. Lederman. 2000. The influence of primary children's ideas in science on teaching practice. *Journal of Research in Science Teaching* 37 (4): 363–385.

American Association for the Advancement of Science (AAAS). 1993. *Benchmarks for Science Literacy.* Washington, DC: National Academies Press.

Baxter, J. 1989. Children's understanding of familiar astronomical events. *International Journal of Science Education* 11 (5): 502–513.

Dove, J. 2000. Does the man in the Moon ever sleep? An analysis of student answers about simple astronomical events: a case study. *International Journal of Science Education* 24 (8): 823–834.

Hannust, T., and E. Kikas. 2007. Children's knowledge of astronomy and its change in the course of learning. *Early Childhood Research Quarterly* 22 (1): 89–104.

Jones, B., P. Lynch, and C. Reesink. 1987. Children's conceptions of the Earth, Sun, and Moon. *International Journal of Science Education* 9 (1): 43–53.

Klein, C. 1982. Children's concepts of the Earth and the Sun: a cross cultural study. *Science Education* 65 (11): 95–107.

Nussbaum, J. 1979. Children's conceptions of the Earth as a cosmic body: A cross-age study. *Science Education* 63 (1): 83–93.

Parker, J., and D. Heywood. 1998. The Earth and beyond: developing primary teachers' understanding of basic astronomical events. *International Journal of Science Education* 20 (5): 503–520.

Schoultz, J., R. Saljo, and J. Wyndhamn. 2001. Heavenly talk: discourse, artifacts, and children's understanding of elementary astronomy. *Human Development* 44 (2–3): 103–118.

Society
and
Science Learning

20

Cultural Diversity in the Science Classroom

By Patrick L. Brown and Sandra K. Abell

"I teach in a growing area that becomes more culturally diverse each year. I am worried that I may not be reaching some of my fifth-grade class in science."

How can cultural perspectives affect students' views of science and science learning?

First, when students come to science class, they bring a variety of perspectives formed in part from their cultural heritage, religious beliefs, and family background. This may create challenges for students whose experiences are different from typical "ways of knowing" promoted in school science. In Texas, Allen and Crawley (1998) studied fifth-grade Kickapoo (Native American) students' science learning. Students focused on their kinship with nature in interpreting their world, which often led to conflicts in science class. Studying Yupiaq children in southwestern Alaska, Kawagley, Norris-

Tull, and Norris-Tull (1998) found that students learned by listening to and mimicking stories that drew on integrated science knowledge. This conflicted with the textbook approach, which divided science into separate, seemingly unconnected, disciplines. Furthermore, the curriculum encouraged students to abandon their traditional worldview of science, which included themselves, nature, and the spiritual world. All students need experiences with school science that connect science with their everyday lives in familiar ways.

Second, students from different cultural backgrounds may have different styles of interaction that make it hard for them to perform in the ways their science teachers expect. In their study of Texas Kickapoo children, Allen and Crawley (1998) found that students viewed science learning as a cooperative venture and wanted to share answers and assignments. To the frustration of their teachers, they viewed their grades in science as a low priority. Anderson, Holland, and Palincsar (1997) found that learning science was difficult for sixth-grade students whose background was different from the language and interaction norms used in school science. For example, when creating a presentation to explain molecules and matter, the students focused on getting along with each other and creating an attractive and well-designed poster, rather than giving priority to learning the science concepts. When student and teacher expectations differ, students may have a more difficult time learning science.

Can inquiry-based instruction help bridge cultural backgrounds and foster science learning success?

The hands-on, minds-on nature of inquiry may help all students develop authentic science interactions and learn science in a context that is meaningful and relevant to their lives. Working with fourth-grade Haitian and Hispanic students, Fradd et al. (2001) investigated how students performed in an inquiry-based curriculum for teaching the water cycle and weather. Although many of the students came from homes where asking questions

and debating was viewed as challenging authority, over time their teachers guided students to understand that questioning and debating are essential features of scientific inquiry. Fradd and Lee (1999) also examined how inquiry-based teaching influenced the fourth graders in developing science and English language skills. They found that by engaging in scientific inquiry, students benefited from working in groups, gained an understanding of the nature of science, and improved their English. In another study, third- and fourth-grade students from various linguistic and cultural groups developed enhanced understanding of science concepts and abilities to do scientific inquiry (asking scientific questions, designing investigations, recording results, and drawing conclusions) by engaging in inquiry (Cuevas et al. 2005). As the above examples reflect, inquiry-based science instruction can indeed be effective in helping all students access the world of science.

How can teachers best support diverse cultural backgrounds when teaching science?

Teachers can help all students learn science by allowing diverse approaches to scientific reasoning in their classrooms. For example, students might use both their first and second languages to engage in science. Jean-Charles, a student in a sixth-grade bilingual classroom, used English to clarify technical terms not present in his first language, Haitian Creole. By expressing his ideas in two languages, he used his full range of linguistic capabilities to develop more in-depth arguments and understanding of metamorphosis in mealworms (Warren et al. 2001). Students might also be encouraged to engage in creative thinking in science. Another student in the bilingual class, Emilio, designed an experiment to test whether ants prefer light or darkness. Unlike the typical science class in which students think about problems from an outsider's perspective, Emilio was encouraged to be creative and to think about being both inside and outside of the ant's habitat while designing his investigation. The interplay of Emilio's imaginative (insider) and evaluative (outsider) perspectives resulted in deeper reasoning about variables and experimental design. By opening up the science class to different languages and types of reasoning, teachers can encourage students to cross borders between their cultural backgrounds and the science classroom.

References

Allen, N. J., and F. E. Crawley. 1998. Voices from the bridge: Worldview conflicts of Kickapoo students of science. *Journal of Research in Science Teaching* 35 (2): 111–132.

Anderson, C. W., D. J. Holland, and A.S. Palincsar. 1997. Canonical and sociocultural approaches to research and reform in science education: The story of Juan and his group. *The Elementary Science Journal* 97 (4): 359–383.

Cuevas, P., O. Lee, J. Hart, and R. Deaktor. 2005. Improving science inquiry with elementary students of diverse backgrounds. *Journal of Research in Science Teaching* 42 (3): 337–357.

Fradd, S. H., and O. Lee. 1999. Teachers' roles in promoting science inquiry with students from diverse language backgrounds. *Educational Researcher* 28 (6): 14–20, 42.

Fradd, S. H., O. Lee, F.X. Sutman, and K. M. Saxton. 2001. Promoting science literacy with English language learners through instructional materials development: A case study. *Bilingual Research Journal* 25 (4): 417–439.

Kawagley, A. O., D. Norris-Tull, and R. A. Norris-Tull. 1998. The indigenous worldview of Yupiaq culture: Its scientific nature and relevance to the practice and teaching of science. *Journal of Research in Science Teaching* 35 (2): 133–144.

Warren, B., C. Ballenger, M. Ogonowski, A. S. Rosebery, and J. Hudicourt-Barnes. 2001. Rethinking diversity in learning science: The logic of everyday sense making. *Journal of Research in Science Teaching* 38 (5): 529–552.

21

ELLs and the Language of School Science

By Mark J. Gagnon and Sandra K. Abell

"I have five English language learners in my class, at various levels of learning English. Should I hold off teaching them science until they are more proficient in English?"

What challenges do English language learners face while learning science?

All students are challenged to bridge the gap between their everyday language and the academic language of school science. In science, everyday words (e.g., *gas, consumer, wave*) take on new and specialized meanings. In science, language denotes the relationship among ideas (e.g., cause/effect; instance/generalization; individual/group member), with features that are often subtle and abstract. Such features of science language make school science difficult for all students. Yet these features complicate matters even more for English language learners (ELLs) who have the added burden of a home language different than English. For example, for much of the new science vocabulary, ELLs do not know the home-language equivalents and may struggle with the English-language definitions. In response, some educators assume that learning English is a prerequisite for learning subject matter like science. Given that ELLs could take 4–10 years to become proficient in academic English (Thomas and Collier 2002), waiting to teach them science is misguided. However, we may need to rethink how we go about teaching these students. When science class includes mainly textbook reading and teacher talk, ELLs find class more difficult (Stoddart et al. 2002). These students need meaningful cues, such as context-based visuals and concrete objects, to help make sense of the textbook or the teacher. Furthermore, they need opportunities to participate in science through their own talk.

How can ELLs develop scientific understanding through science talk?

ELLs benefit when they are given the opportunity to use their everyday home language and everyday English to help explain and justify their scientific ideas. Warren and her colleagues (2001) found that sixth-grade bilingual students used their everyday reasoning, in both English and their home language, as a resource to help them think and develop school science language. Students engaged in a lively conversation as they negotiated the meaning of the term *change* in a unit about life cycles. During the science circle, Jean-Charles used English to communicate a view of change as undifferentiated growth, but later during an interview, he used his first language, Haitian Creole, to distinguish between "growing" and "developing" as he talked about the types of changes that beetles experience. By using both home language and English, Jean-Charles was able to deepen his understanding of life cycles and develop more accurate scientific vocabulary.

How do ELLs benefit from inquiry-based science instruction?

Inquiry-based science instruction offers ELLs opportunities to par-ticipate in and develop the language of school science. Hampton and Rodriquez (2001) found that bilingual K–5 students developed conceptual understanding by manipulating hands-on materials and interacting orally with their peers. Lee and her colleagues (2008) helped teachers in urban settings teach science through inquiry to third-grade students from a variety of language backgrounds. The researchers found that students in the inquiry classrooms scored higher on both science and mathematics achievement tests than students in comparison classrooms. Furthermore, the gap between ELLs and non-ELLs disappeared. These studies demonstrate that all students benefit when they have opportunities to interact with and talk about phenomena in science class.

What strategies are effective in helping ELLs develop the language of school science?

Sheltered instruction (Fathman and Crowther 2006) is a common approach to supporting ELLs. Teachers set goals for both language development and science learning. For example, in a second-grade unit about soils, a teacher might set understanding components of soil as the science objective, and answering questions in simple sentences as the language objective. Teachers can use English labels on science equipment and posters about science processes to reinforce vocabulary and conceptual connections. Teachers can provide a range of support during instruction as well. For example, by probing students for more information, restating students' spoken ideas to clarify their reasoning, asking students to state ideas aloud in choral speaking, or getting students talking in small groups, teachers provide opportunities for students to practice school science language multiple times as they build their science understandings and communicate with higher levels of language (e.g., giving examples to support thinking). During instruction, teachers can also provide nonverbal supports for understanding, such as gestures, pictures, and demonstrations. Teachers might also consider building a series of language opportunities in science.

Gibbons (2002) recommends a sequence where students move from describing firsthand experiences orally to expressing academic science knowledge in writing. For example, fourth graders might build and observe a terrarium, discuss the components of the food web in this habitat, and then write a summary of the interactions within the terrarium. Finally, teachers

can consider equitable ways to write assessment items for ELLs. In a study of grades 6–8, Siegel (2007) found 11 kinds of linguistic, cognitive, and visual modifications to life science test items that improved the performance of ELLs. These modifications include replacing sentences with bulleted items, reducing the number of words in an item, adding visual supports, and matching the language of the item to that of instruction more precisely. In these ways, teachers can help all students in their classrooms learn the language of science.

References

Fathman, A. K., and D. T. Crowther. 2006. *Science for English language learners: K–12 classroom strategies.* Arlington, VA: NSTA Press.

Gibbons, P. 2002. *Scaffolding language, scaffolding learning: Teaching second language learners in the mainstream classroom*. Portsmouth, NH: Heinemann.

Hampton, E., and R. Rodriguez. 2001. Inquiry science in bilingual classrooms. *Bilingual Research Journal* 26 (2): 213–239.

Lee, O., J. Maerten-Rivera, R. D. Penfield, K. LeRoy, and W. G. Secada. 2008. Science achievement of English language learners in urban elementary schools: Results of a first-year professional development intervention. *Journal of Research in Science Teaching* 45 (1): 31–52.

Siegel, M. A. 2007. Striving for equitable classroom assessments for linguistic minorities: Strategies for and effects of revising life science items. *Journal of Research in Science Teaching* 44 (6): 864–881.

Stoddart, T., A. Pinal, M. Latzke, and D. Canaday. 2002. Integrating inquiry science and language development for English language learners. *Journal of Research in Science Teaching* 39 (8): 664–687.

Thomas, W., and V. Collier. 2002. A national study of school effectiveness for language minority students' long-term academic achievement. Santa Cruz, CA, and Washington, DC: Center for Research on Education, Diversity and Excellence.

Warren, B., C. Ballenger, M. Ogonowski, A. Rosebery, and J. Hudicourt-Barnes. 2001. Rethinking diversity in learning science: The logic of everyday language. *Journal of Research in Science Teaching* 38 (5): 529–552.

22

Finding a Place for Girls in Science

By Binaben H. Vanmali and Sandra K. Abell

"Last week I asked my fifth graders about their career aspirations. Many of the boys mentioned science-related careers, but few of the girls did. Is there something I can do to help my students see that success in science is achievable for girls and boys?"

How do girls view themselves in science?

Science education researchers Jones, Howe, and Rua (2000) claim that, in elementary schools, girls and boys are both positive about science, although girls prefer life and social sciences over physical sciences. However, elementary girls tend to perceive their science abilities differently from boys. In particular, girls see themselves as less competent in science. In a study of K–6 students and parents in Iowa, Andre and his colleagues (1999) found that grade 4–6 boys perceived themselves with higher competence in physical sci-

ence than girls, even though girls did not differ from boys in liking science. More interesting were the parents' perceptions. Parents saw science as more important for boys, held higher expectations for their performance, and believed science and math-related jobs were male-dominated. Jovanovic and Steinbach King (1998) examined 165 students in hands-on science classrooms, grades 5–8, using observations and surveys. They found a decrease in science ability perceptions over the school year for girls only. The researchers hypothesize that girls and boys might experience classrooms differently. These studies imply that girls' views of themselves as competent in science might be influenced by parental attitudes and by their access to science in classrooms. Do girls and boys have the same opportunities for learning science in school?

What kinds of experiences do girls have in science classrooms?

In 1994, researchers Myra and David Sadker demonstrated that girls in U.S. schools received less attention from teachers across grade levels and subject areas. Teachers called on boys more, commented more on their work, and praised them more. In an updated version of the book, *Still Failing at Fairness: How Gender Bias Cheats Girls and Boys in School and What We Can Do About It*, Sadker and Zittleman (2009) claim that not much has changed. When researchers focus on interactions in elementary science classrooms in particular, a similar picture emerges. Greenfield (1997) found that, although girls and boys were equally engaged with science equipment, girls received less attention from teachers. Jovanovic and Steinbach King (1998) observed that, in exemplary hands-on science classrooms, boys and girls did not participate equally. Although both were just as likely to engage in active-leading activities in small groups, boys were more likely to manipulate equipment actively, while girls were more likely to assist their groups. Jones, Brader-Araje, and colleagues (2000) studied the interactions that took place in two fifth-grade and three second-grade

science classrooms to understand how students used science tools (such as balances and hand lenses) to build new knowledge. The students in these classrooms were divided into all-girl or all-boy dyads for science activities. The girls followed teacher directions carefully during hands-on activities and did little playing with science tools beyond what was called for by the task. Male students tended to tinker with the tools, using them in inventive and exploratory ways. In female dyads, the interactions with the materials were more cooperative—girls tended to share materials and ideas with each other rather than compete for the materials. These studies demonstrate that teachers have an important role to play in guaranteeing equal access to science learning for girls and boys.

What can teachers do to promote gender equity in science class?

Because teacher expectations and classroom interactions often favor boys in science, teachers need to consider strategies to create gender-inclusive science classrooms, as suggested by researchers Brotman and Moore (2008) and Jones, Howe, and Rua (2000).

Portray science as a subject that everyone can learn, rather than a difficult one. Call on both boys and girls to respond to different types of science questions (Park Rogers and Abell 2008). Celebrate the science successes of girls and boys by displaying their science learning products.

Show girls how their interests, experiences, and ideas align with scientific ideas. Link physical science concepts (e.g., force and motion) with life science contexts (e.g., the circulatory system) to help girls relate to all sciences positively.

Use real-world contexts to emphasize the societal relevance of science. Share current examples in the news of the role of science in addressing problems, such as disease control; cancer treatment; earthquake, tornado, and hurricane monitoring; and endangered species laws.

Encourage girls to become competent with scientific tools and equipment. Encourage equal time in different roles for all group members. Use same-sex groups where students are responsible for different tasks some of the time. Ask students to self-evaluate their contributions to small groups.

Provide opportunities for projects that emphasize collaboration and communication. Develop science lessons that span multiple class periods and require group collaboration to complete. Provide guiding questions to elicit discussion and collaboration, and reinforce communication and teamwork among group members by requiring peer evaluation by group members.

Promote science-related careers for all students, showing examples of women and men in those careers. Display posters, use books, and invite guest speakers to represent women and men in various science careers. Discuss how careers in medicine, engineering, environmental protection, and science research often involve helping others.

These strategies have the potential to make science approachable for all students and may help girls in your classroom find their place in science.

References

Andre, T., M. Whigham, A. Hendrickson, and S. Chambers. 1999. Competency beliefs, positive affect, and gender stereotypes of elementary students and their parents about science versus other school subjects. *Journal of Research in Science Teaching* 36 (6): 719–47.

Brotman, J. S., and F. M. Moore. 2008. Girls and science: A review of four themes in the science education literature. *Journal of Research in Science Teaching* 45 (9): 971–1002.

Greenfield, T. A. 1997. Gender- and grade-level differences in science interest and participation. *Science Education* 81 (3): 259–76.

Jones, M. G., L. Brader-Araje, L. W. Carboni, G. Carter, M. J. Rua, and E. Banilower, and H. Hatch. 2000. Tool time: Gender and students' use of tools, control, and authority. *Journal of Research in Science Teaching* 37 (8): 760–83.

Jones, M. G., A. Howe, and M. J. Rua. 2000. Gender differences in students' experiences, interests, and attitudes toward science and scientists. *Science Education* 84 (2): 180–92.

Jovanovic, J., and S. Steinbach King. 1998. Boys and girls in the performance-based science classroom: Who's doing the performing? *American Educational Research Journal* 35 (2): 477–96.

Park Rogers, M. A., and S. K. Abell. 2008. The art (and science) of teacher questioning. *Science and Children* 46 (2): 54–55.

Sadker, M., and D. Sadker. 1994. *Failing at fairness: How America's schools cheat girls.* New York: Scribner.

Sadker, D., and K. R. Zittleman. 2009. *Still failing at fairness: How gender bias cheats girls and boys in school and what we can do about it.* New York: Simon and Schuster.

23

Societal Issues in Science

By Patrick L. Brown and Sandra K. Abell

"My state standards say that students should be able to use science to make personal and societal decisions. I'm really not sure how to address this goal in my science teaching."

What are the features of science units that use societal issues as organizers?

The key is to start with local contexts in which students use evidence-based reasoning to discuss both science- and nonscience-related issues. Students must be able to weigh sides of an issue, make informed decisions, and see themselves as participating members of the community. For example, Pedretti (1999) investigated fifth- and sixth-grade students' learning of environmental issues associated with building a zinc mine in their community. Students researched zinc mining, investigated mining through an exhibit at a local museum, and presented evidence for their perspectives in a town meeting. Students addressed the balance needed between the environment and the local economy as they stated their positions about whether or not the town should allow the building of the mine. They based their decisions on the knowledge built from their own research and their peers' presentations.

How do students benefit?

When students investigate local issues in science class, they gain research and critical-thinking skills while improving their attitudes toward science. In Hawaii, Volk and Cheak (2003) studied fifth and sixth graders who investigated environmental problems in their community and proposed evidence-based solutions during a community symposium. Teachers noticed that students gained appreciation for different types of resources—books, encyclopedias, newspaper and magazine articles, and minutes of public hearings. Yager and Akcay (2008) studied sixth graders engaged in a science unit in which they investigated the proposed site for a landfill in their town. As a result, students had more positive attitudes toward science, applied science in complex situations, and reported talking about science more in their homes and in the community. Christenson (2004) researched teachers' perceptions of using children's books to teach about industrial development in rain forests and solid waste recycling. First- and second-grade teachers reported that the books helped children develop critical-thinking skills through understanding the multiple perspectives involved with these issues.

How can using societal issues in science foster citizenship education?

Another benefit of using societal issues as curriculum organizers is that students develop lifelong skills, confidence, and motivation to evaluate and act upon issues that affect their lives. Lester et al. (2006) studied fifth-grade students' learning about the relationship between greenhouse gases and global warming. They found that, as students gained knowledge of greenhouse gases, their level of social activism increased. Students recognized that driving less, turning lights off when not in use, planting trees, using solar power, and recycling were actions they could take to decrease global warming. In the Volk and Cheak study (2003), interview data revealed that letting students investigate a local environmental issue prepared them to be active citizens who promoted community awareness. During the unit, some students took statewide actions, gave testimony at the legislature, and published articles in the local newspaper about recycling plastic bottles. Community members and parents who attended their community symposium were impressed with student confidence and knowledge of the subject matter. Farmer, Knapp, and Benton (2007) studied the long-term impacts of fourth-grade students' experiences learning about ecology and air pollution during a field trip to the Great Smoky Mountains National Park. One year after the field trip, students retained knowledge and displayed an ecological awareness of human impacts on the environment. These studies demonstrate that organizing science units around local issues helps prepare students for active participation in society.

How can teachers support students when exploring societal issues in science class?

Critics of using local issues as themes for science units argue that the science content is often neglected. Thus, it is important for teachers to first consider the science learning goals of any unit. Next, teachers can situate the science concepts in a meaningful context. In this chapter's examples, the societal issues were meaningful and relevant to students' lives. In some cases, teachers have used their school yards as outdoor classrooms in which to situate meaningful science learning. For example, Kenney, Militana, and Donohue (2003) showed that elementary teachers could use the school yard to study pollution and prepare students to respect and conserve their local environment. Third, teachers can help students explore societal issues by creating an open and supportive learning environment. Many societal issues are controversial. It is important to create a safe and risk-free classroom climate where students can discuss their ideas, personal needs, experiences, and responsibilities. Some teachers have found it beneficial to include parents in student learning of science through societal issues. In Costa Rica, Vaughan et al. (2003) studied third and fourth graders who were

learning about conservation efforts related to a locally endangered species of bird—the scarlet macaw. Through the use of coloring books, students learned natural history and conservation efforts aimed at the scarlet macaw. Students spent considerable time coloring with and reading their books to their parents, which not only increased their knowledge but also improved parental interest in conservation. Although using societal issues in science class may require time to identify science goals, find appropriate societal contexts, and design authentic learning activities, the benefits for students are many.

References

Christenson, M. A. 2004. Teaching multiple perspectives on environmental issues in elementary classrooms: A story of teacher inquiry. *The Journal of Environmental Education* 34 (4): 3–16.

Farmer, J., D. Knapp, and G. M. Benton. 2007. An elementary school environmental education field trip: Long-term effects on ecological and environmental knowledge and attitude development. *Journal of Environmental Education* 38 (3): 33–42.

Kenney, J. L., H. P. Militana, and M. H. Donohue. 2003. Helping teachers to use their school's backyard as an outdoor classroom: A report on the watershed learning project. *The Journal of Environmental Education* 35 (1): 18–26.

Lester, B. T., L. Ma, O. Lee, and J. Lambert. 2006. Social activism in elementary science education: A science, technology, and society approach to teach global warming. *International Journal of Science Education* 28 (18): 315–39.

Pedretti, E. 1999. Decision making and STS education: Exploring scientific knowledge and social responsibility in schools and science centers through an issues–based approach. *Journal of School Science and Mathematics* 99 (4): 174–81.

Vaughan, C., J. Gack, H. Solorazano, and R. Ray. 2003. The effect of environmental education on school children, their parents, and community members: A study of intergeneration and intercommunity learning. *The Journal of Environmental Education* 34 (3): 12–21.

Volk, T. L., and M. J. Cheak. 2003. The effects of an environmental education program on students, parents, and community. *The Journal of Environmental Education* 34 (4): 12–25.

Yager, R. E., and H. Akcay. 2008. Comparison of student learning outcomes in middle school science classes with an STS approach and a typical textbook dominated approach. *Research in Middle Level Education Online* 31 (7): 1–16.

Developing
as a Teacher

24

Making the Most of Professional Development

By Sandra K. Abell and Michele H. Lee

"My school recently revised our science curriculum. I've been comfortable teaching science in the past, but now I must teach a unit on energy. I don't understand energy concepts, I don't know what is appropriate to teach my fourth graders about energy, and I don't know how to help them learn this topic. I need some professional development!"

What does it mean to develop professionally in science teaching?

Teacher preparation programs help teachers build a foundation for entering the teaching profession. However, learning to teach science cannot be achieved in a mere four years—it is a lifelong endeavor. Teachers continue to learn new science content and new teaching strategies throughout their careers. As professionals, they consistently update their knowledge and skills, reflecting upon and improving· their practice. Professional develop-

ment (PD), in all of its forms, is the key to science teacher learning. And teacher learning is essential for achieving the vision of science education reform captured in national and state standards. Numerous studies have shown that the classroom teacher is the most important factor in student science achievement (NRC 2001). Thus teachers must have opportunities for PD that support their knowledge development in science, science learning, and science teaching. Although PD is directed at teacher learning, the ultimate beneficiaries are the students.

What are characteristics of effective professional development?

As reflected in the NSTA position statement on PD (*www.nsta.org/about/positions/profdev.aspx*), there is a great deal of consensus among researchers and policy makers about what makes PD effective. The best PD helps teachers learn science through inquiry and provides opportunities to apply this learning to their classrooms. Park Rogers and her colleagues (2007) interviewed 72 teachers and 23 PD facilitators involved in nine science and mathematics PD projects about their perceptions of PD. They found that PD participants (K–12) and facilitators agreed that PD is most effective when (1) PD content is relevant and applicable to classrooms; (2) teachers are engaged in learning concepts in a manner similar to how their students will learn; and (3) teachers have opportunities to form collegial relationships with other teachers and with the PD facilitators. In our evaluation of PD projects in Missouri (Abell et al. 2007), we found that critical features of PD include these characteristics plus sustained opportunities for teachers to learn over time, where teacher learning is embedded in the context of science teaching. For example, when teachers design, carry out, and assess lessons in their classrooms and have a chance to reflect on their practice with others, new teaching practices are more likely to take hold. Those who design and offer PD should be responsive to the needs of schools, teachers, and students (Hewson 2007), and those who participate in PD should shop for opportunities that display the qualities of effectiveness.

What kinds of PD help teachers develop professionally in science teaching?

Professional development can start with teachers learning individually. However, teacher learning is enhanced through opportunities for collaboration with other teachers. Several groups of researchers have investigated teacher learning in collaborative settings. For example, Briscoe and Peters (1997) worked with 24 elementary teachers from one school district to assist them in implementing problem-centered learning in science. Teachers attended a three-week summer institute and follow-up sessions during the school year. The researchers found that collaboration among teachers in learning science and pedagogy facilitated change in their science teaching practices. Luft and Pizzini (1998) involved 13 elementary teachers in a yearlong program to experience and implement science problem solving using the Problem-Solving Demonstration Classroom. Seeing another teacher use the problem-solving model led to changes in teachers' use of specific teaching strategies. Lewis (2002) described professional development for Japanese elementary teachers that employed a lesson study approach. By conducting and collaboratively studying each other's lessons about simple machines, teachers learned to recognize children's learning difficulties and improve teaching practice. In each of these cases, teachers gained significantly through interaction with PD facilitators and with their teaching colleagues.

Where do I begin?

Teacher learning is not something that happens overnight; instead it is a careerlong responsibility. Rosebery and Puttick (1998) studied Liz, a fourth- and then sixth-grade teacher, during her beginning years of teaching. The researchers followed Liz for one year and six months, watching her do science in a professional development workshop, teach and reteach science units in her classroom, and examine classroom talk and activity among her students. This study demonstrates that teachers need multiple and varied learning experiences associated with their classroom to make sense of science teaching and learning. Your journey to develop professionally has already begun with your reading of *Perspectives*. Next steps might include attending a science teachers conference in your

state or region, taking courses online or at a local university, or finding a summer workshop to attend. Or you can take matters into your own hands by starting a study group or action research team at your school. You can learn more about how to design PD by reading Loucks-Horsley et al. (2003). Make the most of any of these opportunities to learn by garnering the support of your principal and getting together colleagues who can motivate each other long after the workshop or course ends.

References

Abell, S., F. Arbaugh, M. Ehlert, J. Lannin, R. Marra, K. Hutchins, Y.W. Cheng, Z. Kaymaz, M. Lee, D. Merle, and C. Y. Wang. 2007. Evaluation of professional development projects: Missouri department of higher education improving teacher quality grants cycle 4 external evaluation report. Columbia, MO: MU Science Education Center (Available online at *www.pdeval.missouri.edu*)

Briscoe, C., and J. Peters 1997. Teacher collaboration across and within schools: Supporting individual change in elementary science teaching. *Science Education* 81: 51–65.

Hewson, P. 2007. Teacher professional development in science. In *Handbook*

of research on science education,
eds. S. K. Abell and N. G. Lederman,
1179–1203. Mahwah, NJ: Lawrence
Erlbaum Associates.

Lewis, C. C. 2002. Everywhere I looked—
levers and pendulums. *Journal of
Staff Development* 23 (3): 59–65.

Loucks-Horsley, S., N. Love, K. Stiles,
S. Mundry, and P. Hewson. 2003.
*Designing professional development
for teachers of science and
mathematics.* 2nd ed. Thousand
Oaks, CA: Corwin Press.

Luft, J. A., and E. L. Pizzini. 1998. The
demonstration classroom in-service:
Changes in the classroom. *Science
Education* 82: 147–162.

National Research Council. 2001.
*Educating teachers of science,
mathematics, and technology: New
practices for the new millennium.*
Washington, DC: National Academies
Press.

Park Rogers, M., S. Abell, J. Lannin, C.
Wang, K. Musikul, D. Barker, and S.
Dingman. 2007. Effective professional
development in science and
mathematics education: Teachers'
and facilitators' views. *International
Journal of Science and Mathematics
Education* 5: 507–532.

Rosebery, A. S., and G. M. Puttick. 1998.
Teacher professional development
as situated sense-making: A case
study in science education. *Science
Education* 82 (6): 649–677.

25

The Art (and Science) of Asking Questions

By Meredith Park Rogers and Sandra K. Abell

"I struggle with facilitating science conversations in my classroom. Sometimes I ask a question and get only blank stares in return. How can I change my questioning to improve my students' science learning?"

Why do teachers ask questions in science class?

Questions serve as formative assessments that provide information to teachers about student learning in relation to curricular goals. For example, if a teacher wants to check to see if a student has retained a particular fact in science, she might ask a question that narrows answers down to the right one (e.g., *What gas is produced during photosynthesis?*). If a teacher wants to delve deeper to check for conceptual understanding, she might ask a question that requires higher-levels of thinking: *How do you think this little seed became* that big tree? Where do you think all the extra mass came from? (Harvard-Smithsonian Center for Astrophysics 1995). If a teacher wants to help students build conceptual understanding over time, she might tailor a series of questions that move students from recalling prior ideas; to focusing on a phenomenon; to predicting, applying, and explaining (Newton 2002).

In addition to helping students build science concepts, teacher questions can help develop scientific habits of mind. According to the National Science Education Standards, "Teachers ought to ask 'what counts?' What data do we keep? What data do we discard? What patterns exist in the data? Are these patterns appropriate for this inquiry? What explanations account for the patterns? Is one explanation better than another?" (NRC 2000, p. 18).

How do teacher questions promote student thinking in science?

The kinds of questions that teachers ask can open elementary classrooms to scientific thinking. Gallas (1995) worked with first and second graders to facilitate "science talks." She found that her open-ended questions helped spark discussion and the generation of more questions by the students. In a study of 600 elementary students in England, Newton (2002) found that children had a greater chance of understanding scientific ideas about light when they were asked a series of tailored questions that required them to reason about variables, see cause-and-effect relationships, and apply their understanding than if they were asked factual questions alone. Van Zee and a group of teachers, including two primary teachers, an upper elementary teacher, and a high school physics teacher, studied teacher and student questioning in the science class (van Zee et al. 2001). By examining the science talk in their own classrooms, they found that the kinds of questions teachers asked influenced the nature of student thinking. Teacher questions elicited student experiences with a phenomenon, helped students clarify their explanations and consider other points of view, and led students to make sense of their own and others' ideas. The teachers also found that "practicing silence" by refraining from asking questions helped students refine their science ideas.

What kinds of questions work best?

Elstgeest (2001) and Newton (2002) claim that the art of good questioning in science is knowing how to ask the right question at the right time. The right type of question helps students go beyond factual recall to use higher-order thinking skills as they see patterns, make predictions, evaluate evidence, and construct explanations. Elstgeest (2001) explains that the right question "asks children to show rather than to say the answer." This can be accomplished by asking *productive* questions that request students to think and do, not merely remember. The forms of productive questions Elstgeest recommends include attention-focusing (*Have you seen?* or *Do you notice?*), measuring and counting (*How many, how long, and how often?*), comparison (*In what ways are these alike/different? How did you decide to classify these?*), action (*What will happen if … ?*), and problem posing (*Can you find a way to … ?*). Newton (2002) suggests a tailored sequence of questions to help students understand a phenomenon. For example, in a study of light, the teacher might start by tapping into prior knowledge (*How does light leave a flashlight?*), move to drawing attention to significant variables (*What happens to the light as you move the flashlight closer to the wall?*), then ask students to reason causally (*Why do you think the light area gets smaller?*) and to apply their thinking to a new situation (*Why might a driver not see a deer in front of the car?*).

How can you become a better questioner?

In addition to knowing which questions to ask, there is also an art to delivery modes that engage a majority of students and get them thinking. Tobin, Tippins, and Gallard (1994) reviewed many research studies and found overwhelming evidence that giving appropriate wait time after asking questions can promote higher-level thinking and get more students involved in answering. Using the ideas from the research cited in this column, here are a few key steps toward becoming a better questioner.

- Consider your learning outcomes for the science lesson and think about the *right* kind of question to help you reach those outcomes.

- Practice asking *productive* questions that are *tailored* to promote higher levels of thinking.

- Create opportunities for students to ask their own scientific questions by asking more open-ended questions.

- Ask students to answer questions in their notebooks or small groups to give more students a chance to respond.

- Practice wait time and silence.

Adding these steps to your science teaching repertoire will lead to the kind of communication the National Science Education Standards recommend for inquiry-based science classrooms (NRC 2000). Doing so will involve students in higher levels of thinking that have been shown to improve science learning (Treagust 2007).

References

Elstgeest, J. 2001. The right question at the right time. In *Primary science: Taking the plunge*, ed. W. Harlen, 25–35. Portsmouth, NH: Heinemann.

Gallas, K. 1995. *Talking their way into science: Hearing children's questions and theories, responding with curricula.* New York: Teachers College Press.

Harvard-Smithsonian Center for Astrophysics. 1995. *Private Universe Project in Science*. [Motion picture documentary series]. Available from Annenberg Media, 1301 Pennsylvania Avenue, NW #302, Washington, DC 20004

National Research Council (NRC). 2000. *Inquiry and the National Science Education Standards: A guide for teaching and learning*. Washington, DC: National Academies Press.

Newton, L. D. 2002. Questions that help children understand elementary science. *Investigating* 18 (2): 6–9.

Tobin, K. D. J. Tippins, and A. J. Gallard. 1994. Research on instructional strategies for teaching science. In *Handbook of research on science teaching and learning,* ed. D. L. Gabel, 45–93. New York: Macmillan.

Treagust, D. 2007. General instructional methods and strategies. In *Handbook of research on science education,* eds. S. K. Abell and N. G. Lederman, 373–391. Oxford, UK: Taylor and Francis.

van Zee, E. H., M. Iwasyk, A. Kurose, D. Simpson, and J. Wild. 2001. Student and teacher questioning during conversations about science. *Journal of Research in Science Teaching* 38 (2): 159–190.

26

Action Research: Inquiring Into Science Teaching and Learning

By Sandra K. Abell

"My colleague has been raving about her study group—because of it, she is doing research in her classroom about student science learning. That word research *seems intimidating to me, yet I am intrigued by the possibilities."*

Why should I be interested in action research?

Teachers and schools are required by the No Child Left Behind Act to use research-based instructional practices. Although we often think of research as something university professors do, teachers can contribute to the research base on effective instruction by conducting research in their own classrooms. This may seem intimidating on the surface, yet teaching by its very nature is an inquiry-oriented process. Teachers try out various strategies to see what works with their students. They collect evidence of student learning and make instructional decisions based on that

evidence. More importantly, teachers have unique insight into classrooms and can explore questions that are not accessible to "outsiders" like university researchers. For example, when I was coteaching a fifth-grade science class with Marie Roth, we were surprised during a classroom discussion to find students who seemed to misunderstand the model of trophic levels that we had derived from their study of a classroom eco-system. By analyzing video footage of the discussion and examining student drawings from a later lesson, we were able to learn about how students make sense of scientific models and rethink our future instruction (Abell and Roth 1995). We were conducting action research about science teaching and learning!

What is action research?

According to university teacher educators who have encouraged teachers to be researchers, teacher research is intentional and systematic inquiry into classrooms (Cochran-Smith and Lytle 1993). Although teachers embed elements of research such as formative assessment and reflection on practice into their everyday teaching, teacher research is qualitatively different in that it involves the intentional act of setting out to answer a particular question through the systematic analysis of various kinds of data (Roberts, Bove, and van Zee 2007). For example, first-grade teacher Ginger Stovall conducted a study of students' ideas about animals by interviewing each of her students (Stovall and Nesbit 2003). When we add the word *action* to describe research done by teachers, the implication is that, as a result of inquiry into classrooms, teachers will take action to improve their instruction. Stovall used what she had found out about student ideas about animals to plan interventions that would challenge their misconceptions. In another action research project, kindergarten teacher Marletta Iwasyk (1997) investigated student discussions of shadows. What she found encouraged her future actions: "making a special effort to draw in the 'quiet ones' and encourage student leaders to do the same" (p. 46).

I have found that many teachers fear the word *research* until they find that action research questions originate from their own classroom wonderings; that research designs do not have to include control and experimental groups; and that data sources can include observing, listening, and examining student work (Abell, Smith, and Volkmann 2004).

What are the potential benefits and pitfalls?

Benefits from action research include improving both teacher and student learning and adding to the research base about science instruction. Roth (2007) examined 19 studies of teacher learning among individuals engaged in action research and concluded that doing action research is a powerful form of professional development. When teachers take actions based on their research findings, it is logical that student science learning should also benefit. For example, Phyllis Whitin (Whitin and Whitin 1997) tells how she helped her students learn to observe more carefully while carrying out a study of student learning in a fourth-grade classroom. Although much action research is meant to benefit only the teacher researcher or be shared with a small study group, a number of teacher researchers have shared their findings with a national audience (e.g., Roberts, Bove, and van Zee 2007). Their action research has generated knowledge that benefits others. For example, classroom teacher Karen Gallas (1995) documented the progress that first- and second-grade students made in their science talks over an entire year and published a book about her research that has helped other teachers implement science talks in their classrooms.

Even with these potential benefits in mind, action research can be problematic. Being both a teacher and a researcher takes time and can involve conflicting goals. For example, the aim of a teacher researcher in conducting an interview might be to understand how a student thinks about a particular science concept, while the aim of the teacher in the same situation might be to help the student learn that concept. Teacher researchers have to recognize when their research conflicts with their teaching. They can learn how to cope with conflicts by reading studies by teacher researchers who have successfully negotiated both roles in their classrooms. Of bigger concern is the quality of the action research itself. Roth (2007) analyzed 78 published science action research studies. She found that most teacher research

findings led to validating instructional practices rather than confronting the status quo. For action research to be most effective at catalyzing change, researchers must look deeply into student learning and challenge themselves to continually question and improve their instruction.

How do I get started?

If you are intrigued by the possibilities of action research and want ideas about next steps, I recommend learning from those who have preceded you. Several good books about the action research process give ideas for developing research questions, collecting and analyzing data, and sharing the results (e.g., Hubbard and Power 2003). Articles and books published by teacher researchers (like the ones cited in this chapter) can serve as models for your own action research. Many successful teacher researchers have been a part of a study group in their schools or districts (e.g., Fix et al. in Roberts, Bove, and van Zee 2007). Other teacher researchers have formed close partnerships with university researchers (Abell and Roth 1995; Stovall and Nesbit 2003; Whitin and Whitin 1997). I encourage you to find like-minded others who can support you through the action research process.

References

Abell, S. K., and M. Roth. 1995. Reflections on a fifth grade life science lesson: Making sense of children's understanding of scientific models. *International Journal of Science Education* 17 (1): 59–74.

Abell, S. K., D. C. Smith, and M. J. Volkmann. 2004. Inquiry in teacher education. In *Scientific inquiry and the nature of science: Implications for teaching, learning, and teacher education* eds. L. B. Flick and N. G. Lederman. pp. 173–199. Dordrecht, The Netherlands: Kluwer.

Cochran-Smith, M., and S. L. Lytle. 1993. *Inside/outside: Teacher research and knowledge.* New York: Teachers College Press.

Gallas, K.1995. *Talking their way into science: Hearing children's questions and theories, responding with curricula.* New York: Teachers College Press.

Hubbard, R. S., and B. M. Power. 2003. The art of classroom inquiry: A handbook for teacher-researchers. 2nd ed. Portsmouth, NH: Heinemann.

Iwasyk, M. 1997. Kids questioning kids: "Experts" sharing. *Science and Children* 35 (1): 42–46.

Roberts, D., C. Bove, and E. van Zee. 2007. *Teacher research: Stories of learning and growing.* Arlington, VA: NSTA Press.

Roth, K. J. 2007. Science teachers as researchers. In *Handbook of research on science education,* eds. S. K. Abell and N. G. Lederman. pp. 1203–1250. London: Routledge.

Stovall, G., and C. R. Nesbit. 2003. Let's try action research! *Science and Children* 40 (5): 44–48.

Whitin, P., and D. J. Whitin. 1997. *Inquiry at the window: Pursuing the wonders of learners.* Portsmouth, NH: Heinemann.

27

Mentoring New Teachers

By Deborah L. Hanuscin and Michele H. Lee

"Our school has hired four beginning teachers who will start in the fall. We want them to feel welcome and become part of our science teaching community. How can we be effective mentors as we work together with our new colleagues?"

What does research say about mentoring?

Beginning teachers have much to learn about teaching (Odell 1990), including navigating their own classrooms and learning new school procedures and policies. Mentors can assist beginning teachers in making the difficult transition from student to teacher. Smith and Ingersoll (2004) examined data from a national survey and found that beginning teachers who had the support of mentors and well-planned induction programs experienced increased job satisfaction and self-efficacy. In addition, when mentors and mentees had similar teaching assignments and common planning time, new teach-

ers were more likely to remain in the profession.

How does mentoring benefit new teachers?

Mentoring can be a vehicle to support and inspire new teachers' professional development. Beginning teachers profit from instructional guidance as they establish their own set of teaching practices. Appleton and Kindt (2002) followed 20 beginning elementary teachers into their first year of teaching and found that the support of mentors allowed new teachers to engage in practices, such as inquiry, that they might otherwise not have attempted. Above all, the researchers claimed, with the aid of mentors, beginning teachers were able to resolve their most pressing perceived difficulties and develop a vision of the kind of teacher they wanted to be. As new teachers negotiate the "reality shock" of initial teaching experiences (Tauer

1998), they benefit from mentors who provide important information about school procedures and guidelines, and emotional support. Without this support, researchers have noted that beginning teachers may rely on highly teacher-centered instruction and less effective teaching methods (Odell 1990; Appleton and Kindt 2002; Feiman-Nemser 2001).

How do experienced teachers benefit from serving as mentors?

The value of mentoring is not limited to new teachers; experienced teachers also benefit by serving as mentors. Odell (1990) reviewed the research on mentoring and identified such benefits to mentors as increasing their awareness of their own professional development and developing a clearer justification for their own teaching practices. Tauer (1998) examined the experiences of 10 mentor teachers in a districtwide mentoring program (K–8) and the impacts of successful mentor–mentee relationships. She reported that teachers viewed their mentorship as a way to contribute to the profession and repay the mentors who helped them during their first years of teaching. Serving as a mentor was a source of both professional and personal development for these teach-

ers, as it encouraged them to reflect on their own teaching practices.

What does effective mentoring look like?

There is not one single image of effective mentoring. Mentors assume a variety of roles, including those they believe they should assume and those that mentees ask them to assume. The literature on mentoring describes mentors acting as parent figures (protecting the mentee from serious difficulty but at the same time allowing them to learn from mistakes); support systems (supporting and helping the mentee on a day-to-day basis and in moments of crisis); troubleshooters (helping the mentee head off trouble); colleagues (fellow learner); "scaffolders" (sharing experiences and knowledge of ways to work with students, design curriculum, and solve classroom problems—moving beyond basic support to specific help on how to teach); master teachers (providing role models); and coaches (providing training to new teachers) (Abell et al. 1995; Odell 1990). In studying mentor–mentee pairs, Tauer (1998) noted successful mentoring includes: (1) maintenance of a long-term interaction between the novice and experienced teacher; (2) a structured relationship honoring the needs, wants, or expectations of the new teacher; and (3) common goals and similar images of what the relationship should be. Both novice and experienced teachers must build consensus and constantly reassess the purpose of their relationship.

How can I be an effective mentor?

Effective mentoring works best when mentors and mentees share a vision of good teaching. Feiman-Nemser (2001) examined the mentoring approach of Pete Frazer, a 30-year veteran teacher who was widely recognized as an outstanding mentor. Pete was released from the classroom to work full-time with beginning elementary teachers. By studying Pete's interactions with mentees, Feiman-Nemser learned that effective mentors are adept at (1) finding openings to discuss problems of practice focused on issues central to good teaching; (2) enabling new teachers to pinpoint problems that stem from ineffective instruction and/ or management; (3) probing novices' thinking about their students and their work; (4) noticing and providing specific feedback regarding signs of growth and progress; (5) helping focus beginning teachers' attention on student thinking; (6) helping new teachers make meaningful connections between theory and practice;

(7) thinking aloud so that beginning teachers can better understand how they think about particular tasks and problems; and (8) modeling inquiry within their own practice.

While teaching experience is often viewed as sufficient for serving as a mentor, researchers argue that training is essential to successful mentoring programs (Tauer 1998). Both mentees and mentors should show a willingness to explore their teaching and a desire to improve their teaching practices. The NSTA position statement on induction programs for the support and development of beginning teachers of science (NSTA 2007) supports this notion and provides the following suggestions:

- Be aware that mentees have different needs and abilities, and be prepared to work with teachers at different levels and with different areas of expertise and understanding.

- Coordinate your own work with mentees with other people and programs that are serving them.

- Help build the capacity of the new teacher by presenting science content accurately and effectively, reinforcing appropriate pedagogical practices, providing information pertaining to safety, and supporting essential instructional processes, including the use of inquiry in the classroom.

- Provide logistical assistance, such as showing the location of science supplies, helping the teacher acquire materials or resources, offering suggestions about science instruction, and orienting the new teacher of science to the environment of the school.

References

Abell, S. K., D. R. Dillon, C. J. Hopkins, W. D. McInerney, and D. G. O'Brien. 1995. "Somebody to count on": Mentor/intern relationships in a beginning teacher internship program. *Teaching and Teacher Education* 11 (2): 173–188.

Appleton, K., and I. Kindt. 2002. Beginning elementary teachers' development as teachers of science. *Journal of Science Teacher Education* 13 (1): 43–61.

Feiman-Nemser, S. 2001. Helping novices learn to teach: Lessons from an exemplary support teacher. *Journal of Teacher Education* 52 (1): 17–30.

National Science Teachers Association (NSTA). 2007. NSTA position statement: Induction programs for the support and development of beginning teachers of science. Available online at *www.nsta.org/about/positions/induction.aspx*.

Odell, S. J. 1990. *Mentor teacher programs: What research says to the teacher.* Washington, DC: National Education Association.

Smith, T. M., and R. M. Ingersoll. 2004. What are the effects of induction and mentoring on beginning teacher turnover? *American Educational Research Journal* 41 (3): 681–714.

Tauer, S. M. 1998. The mentor-protégé relationship and its impact on the experienced teacher. *Teaching and Teacher Education* 14 (2): 205–218.

Index

Index

Index

Index

Index